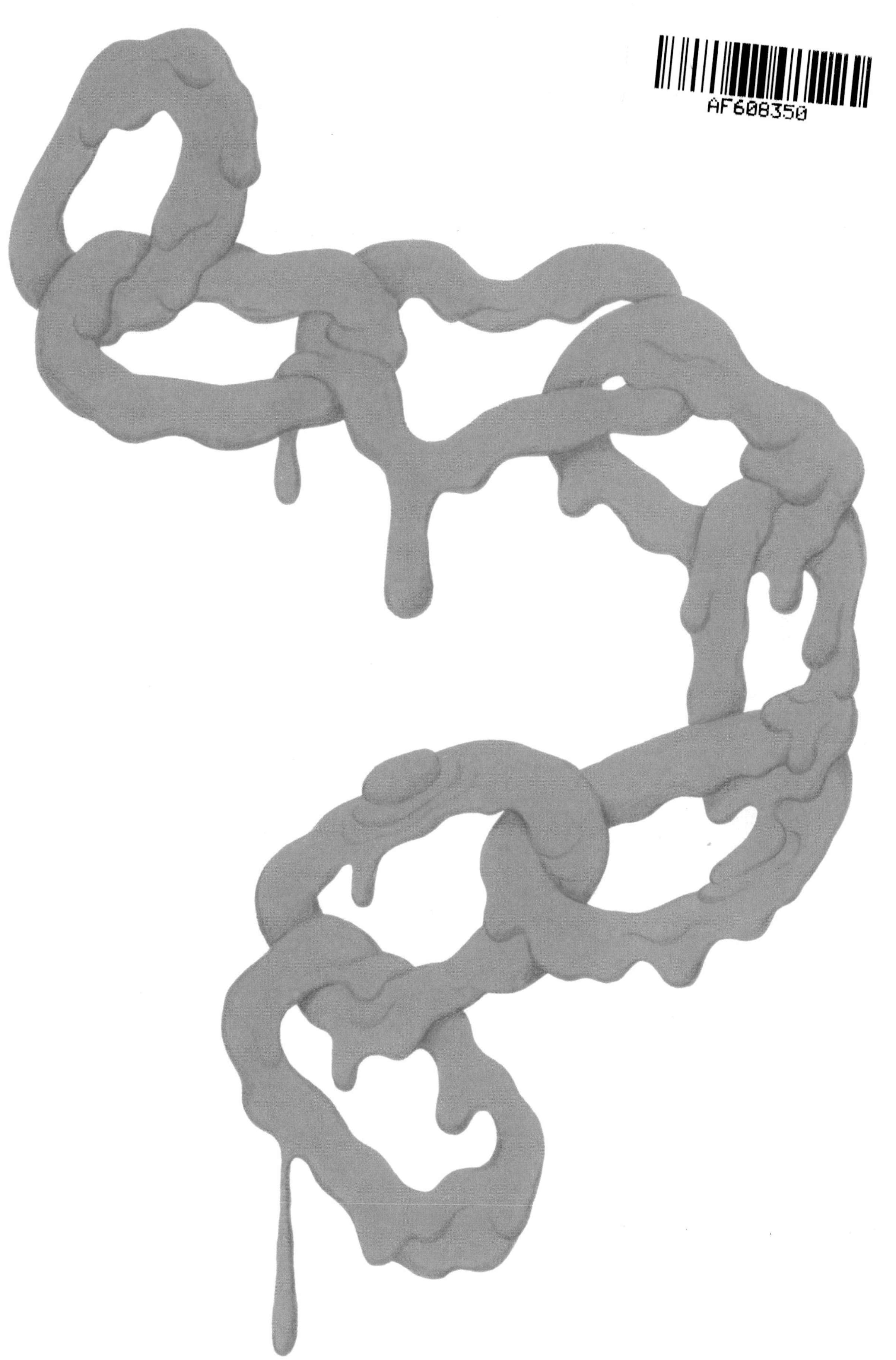

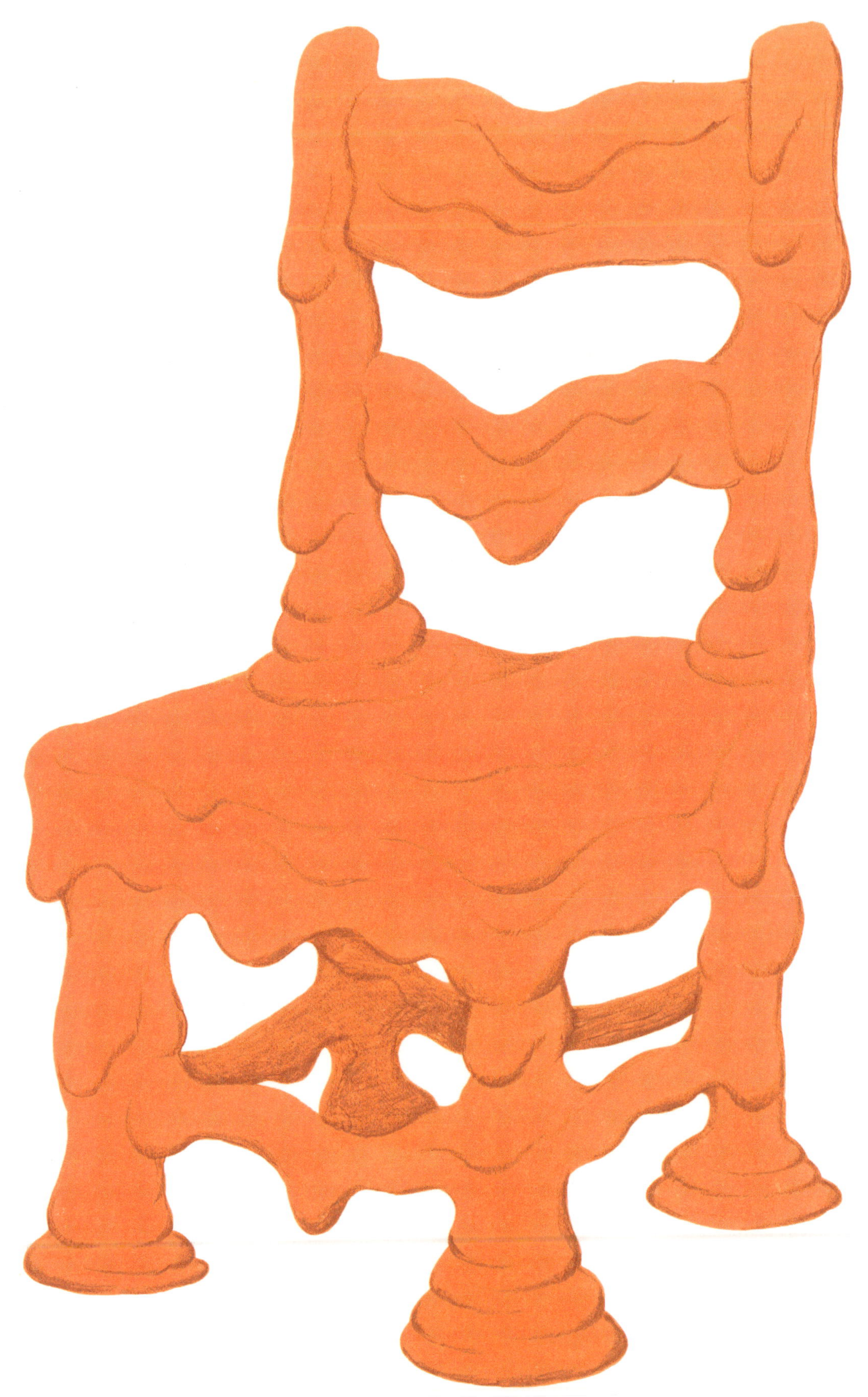

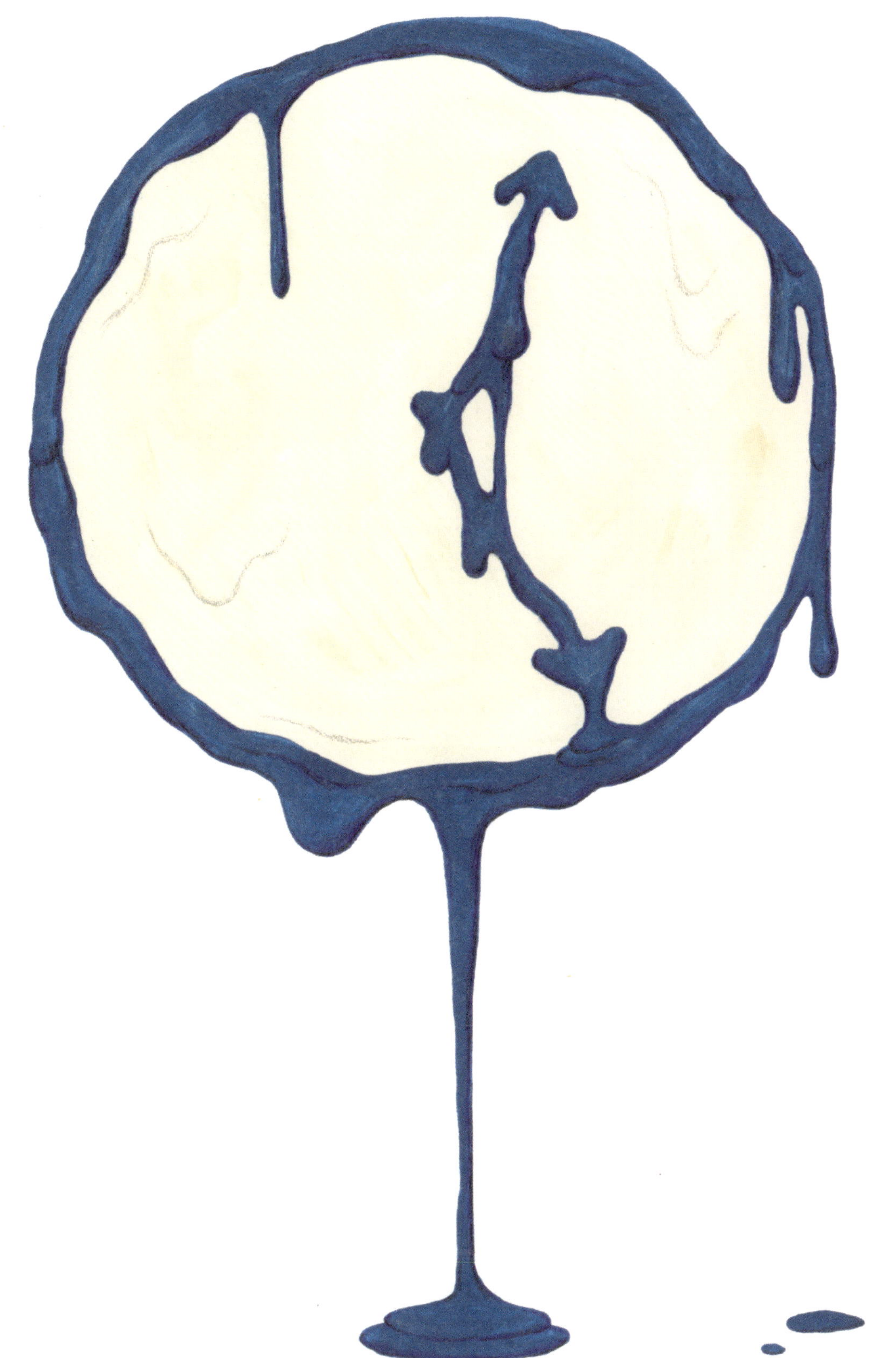

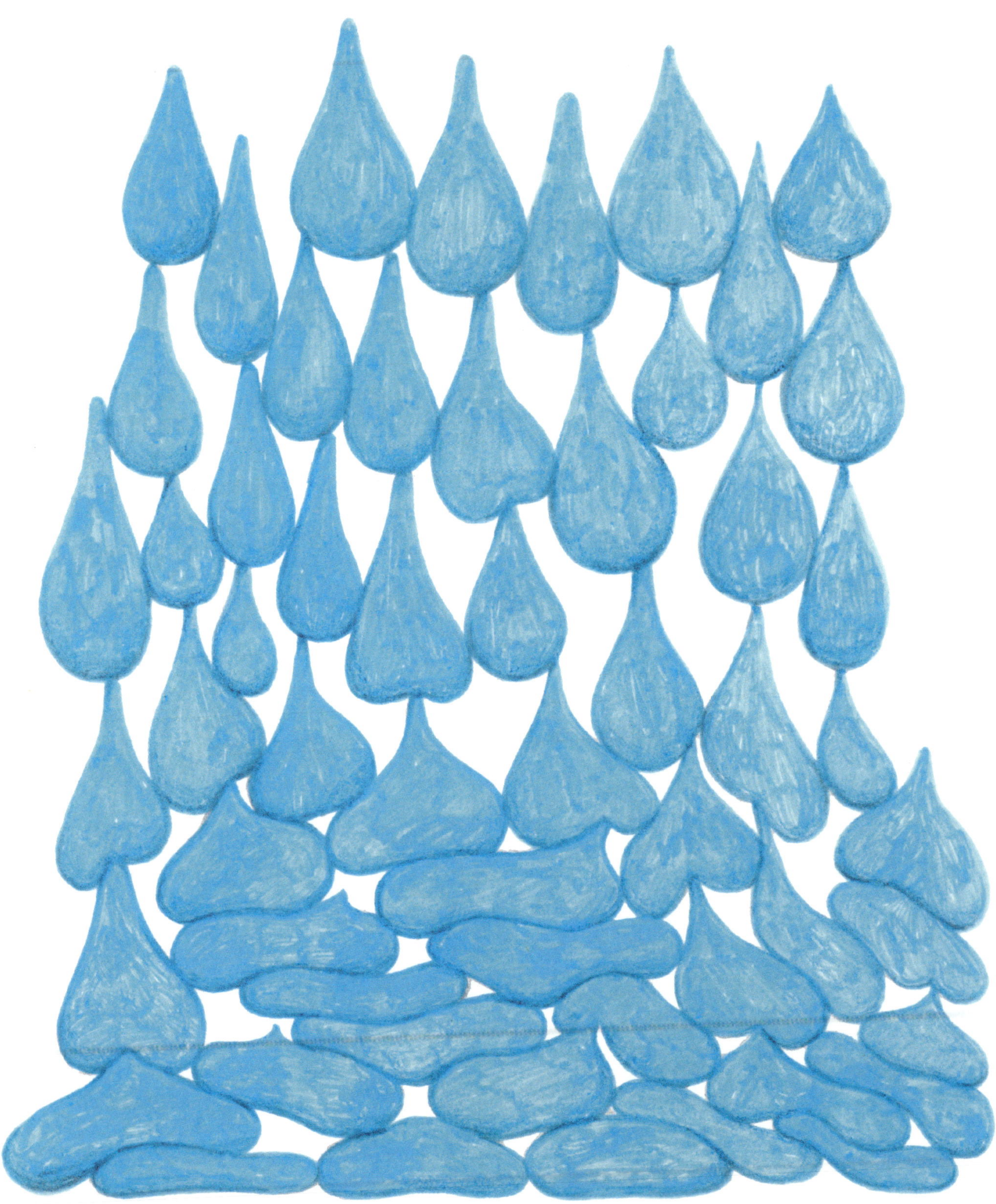

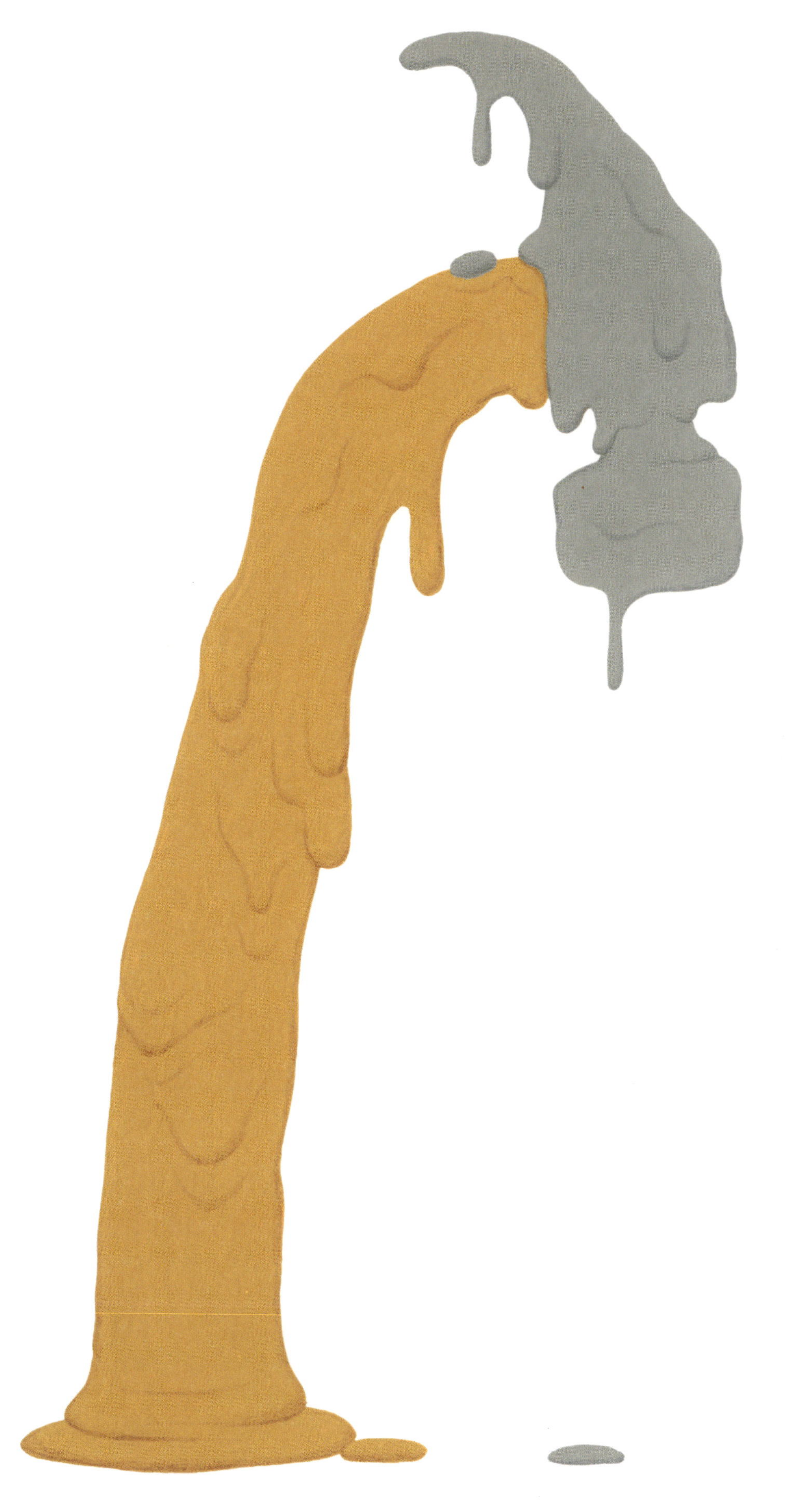

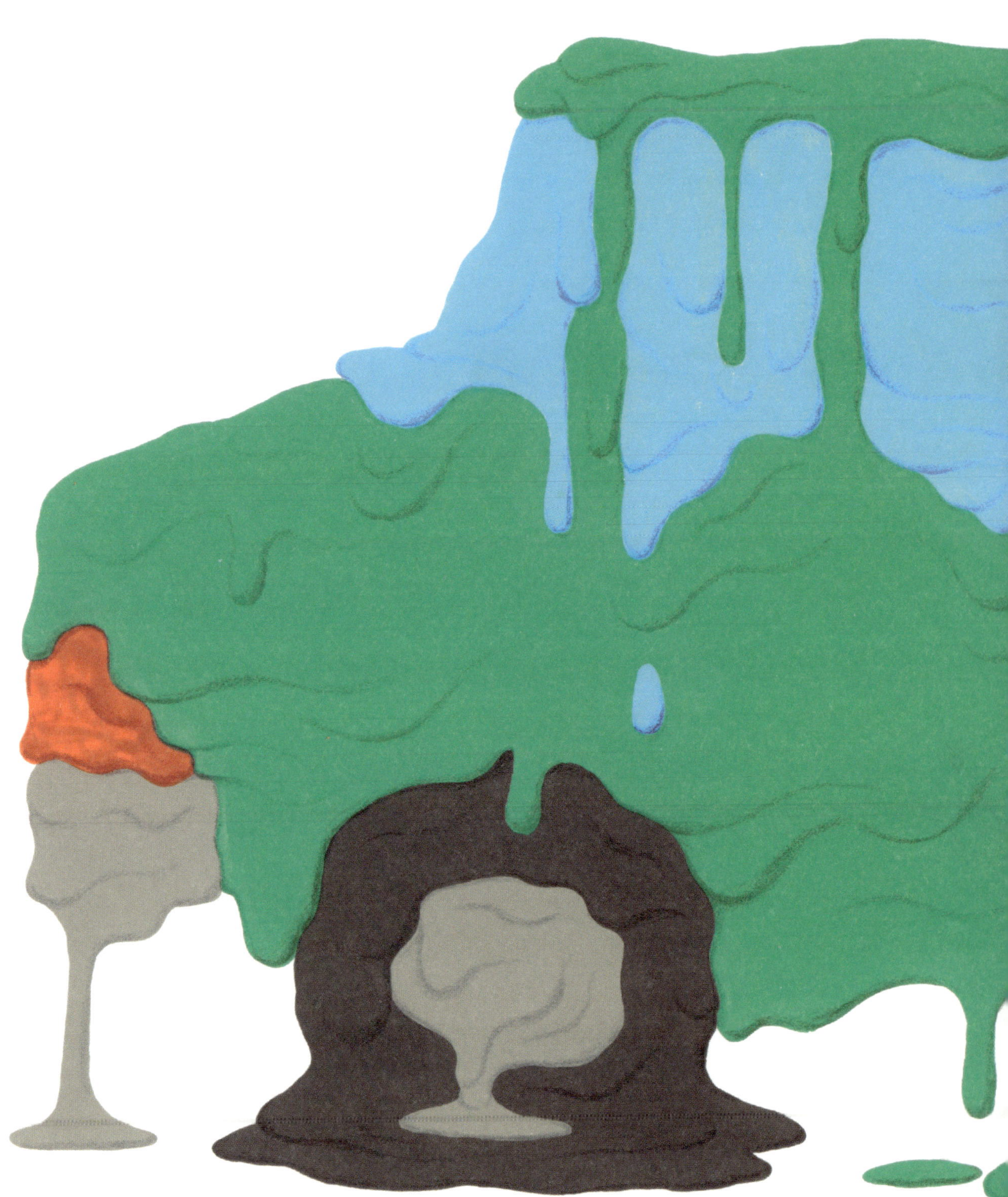

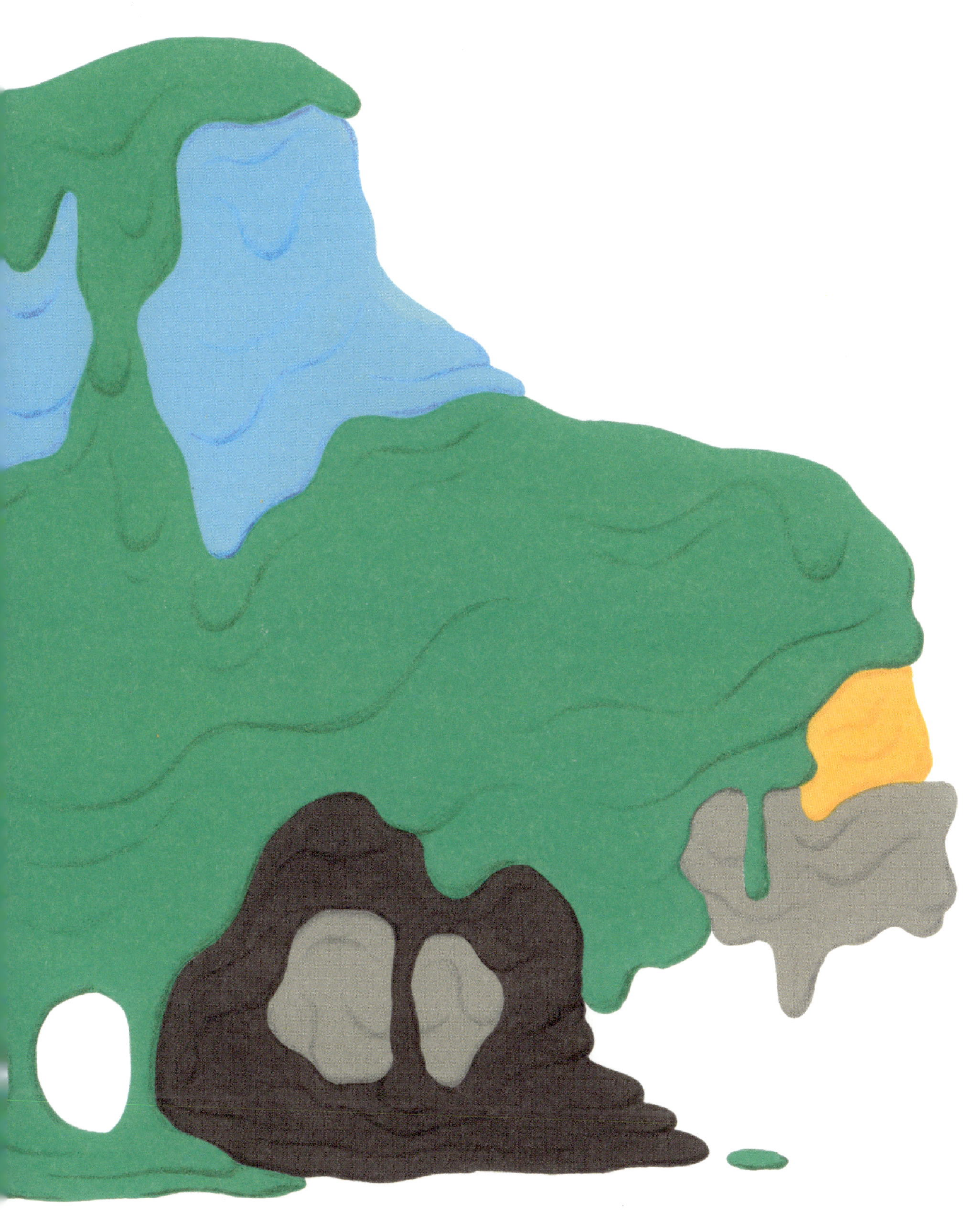

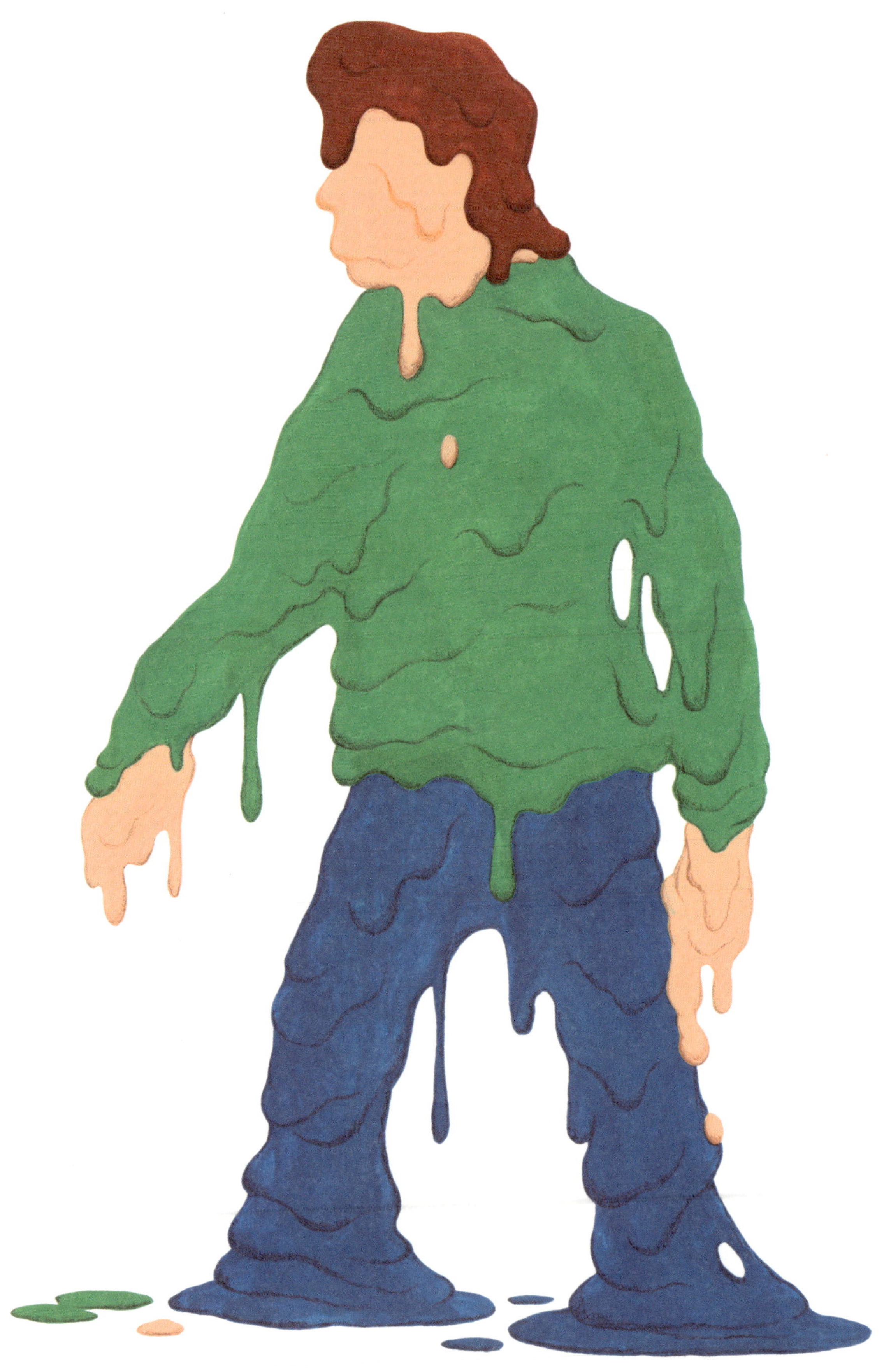

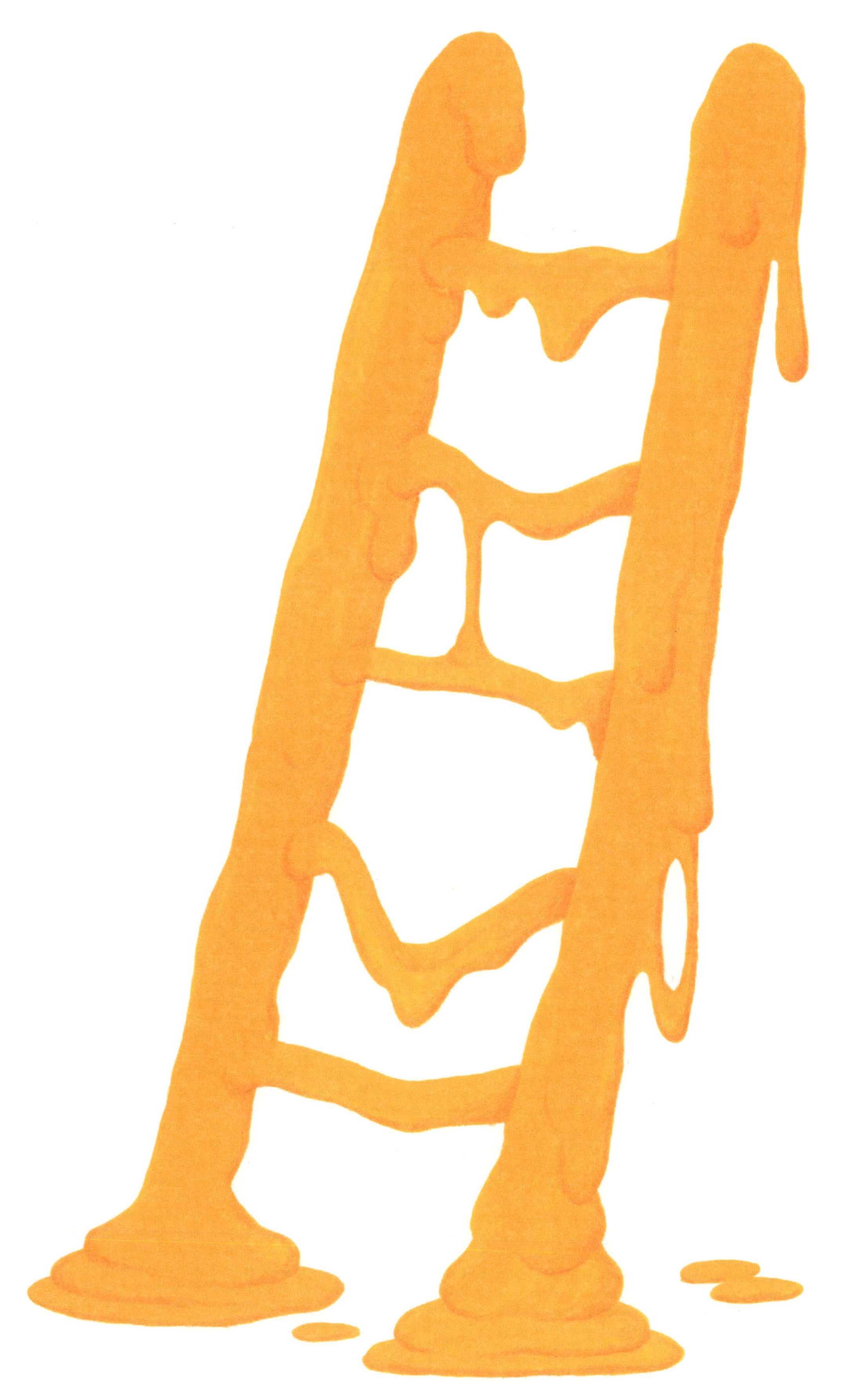

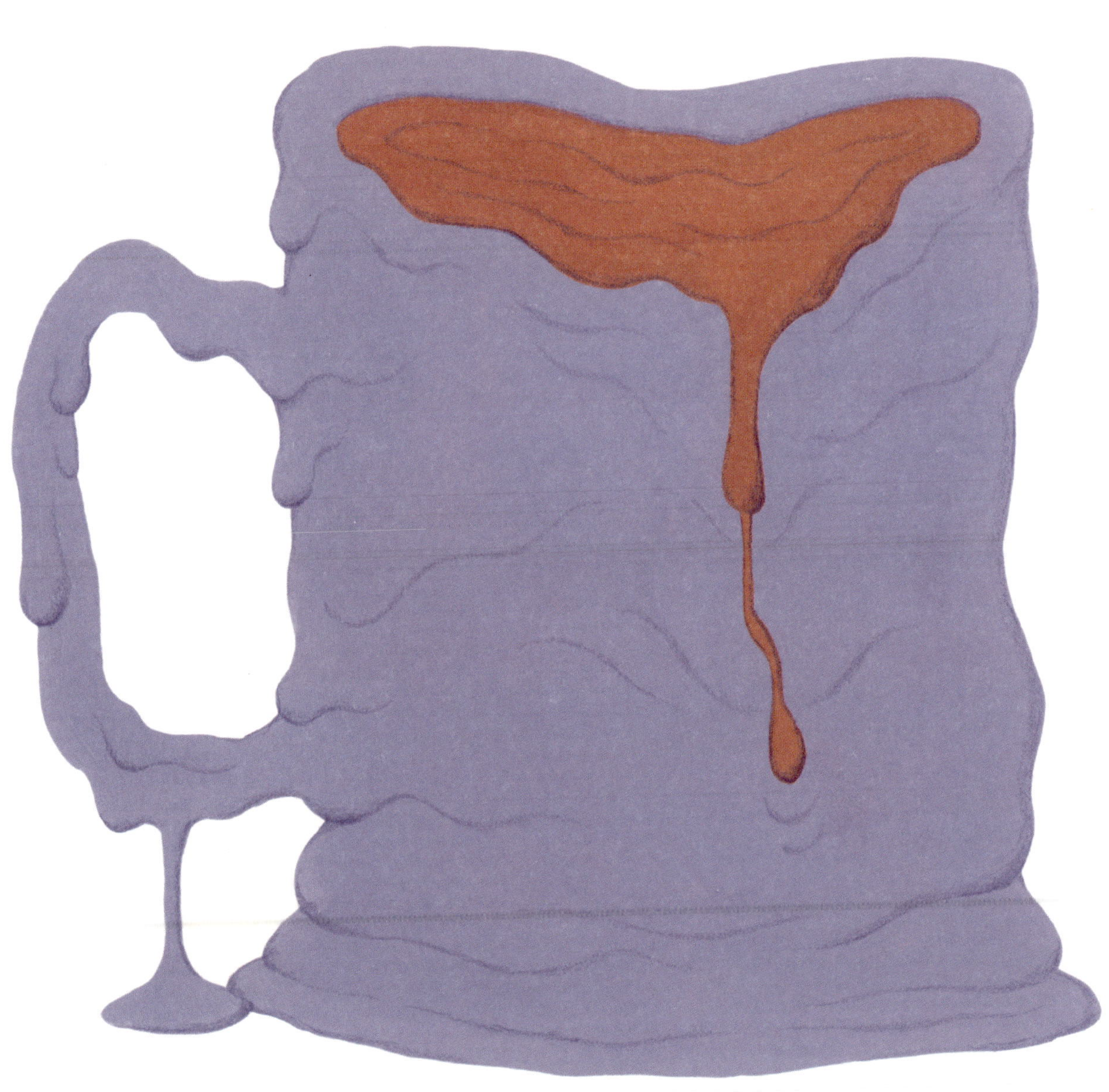

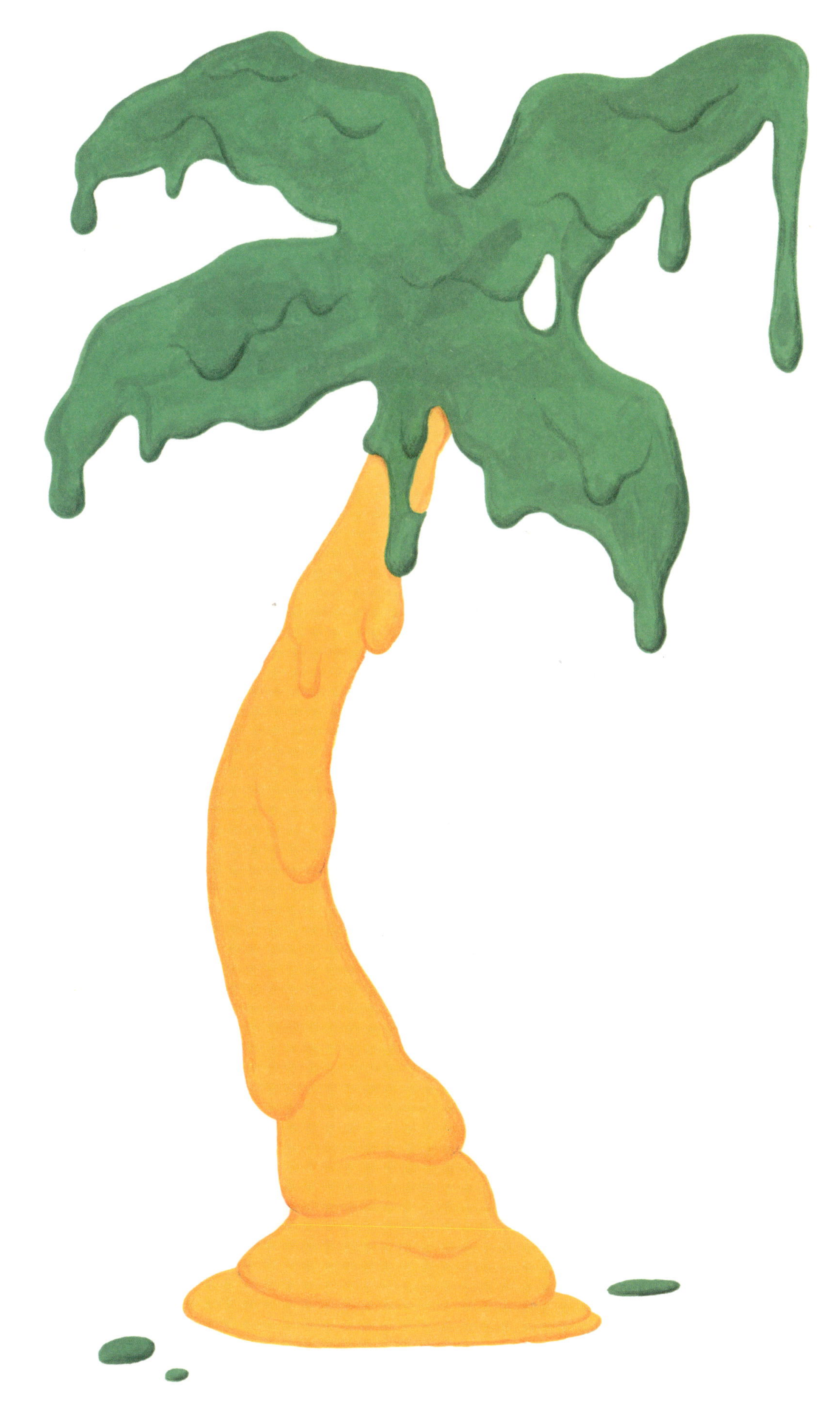

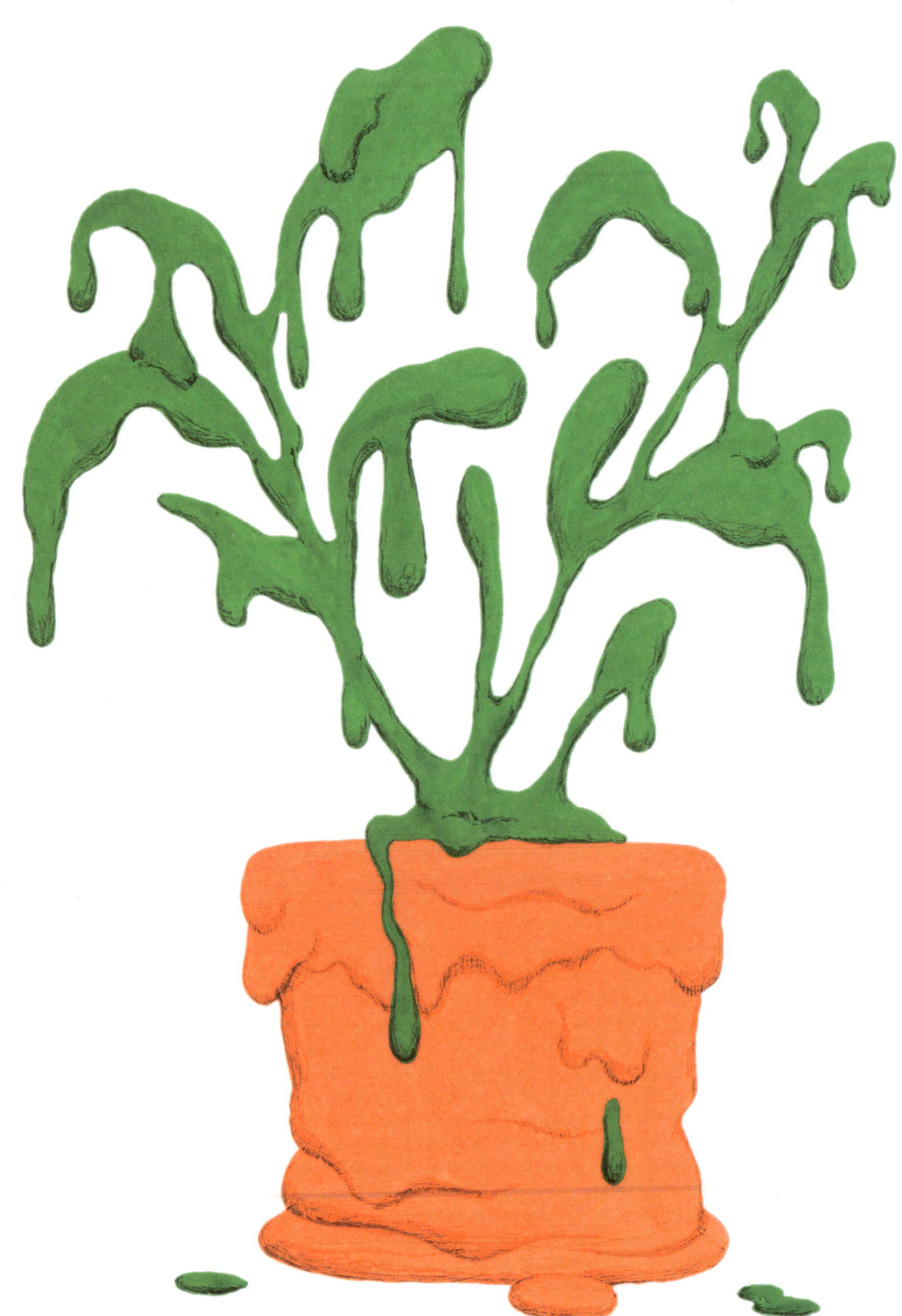

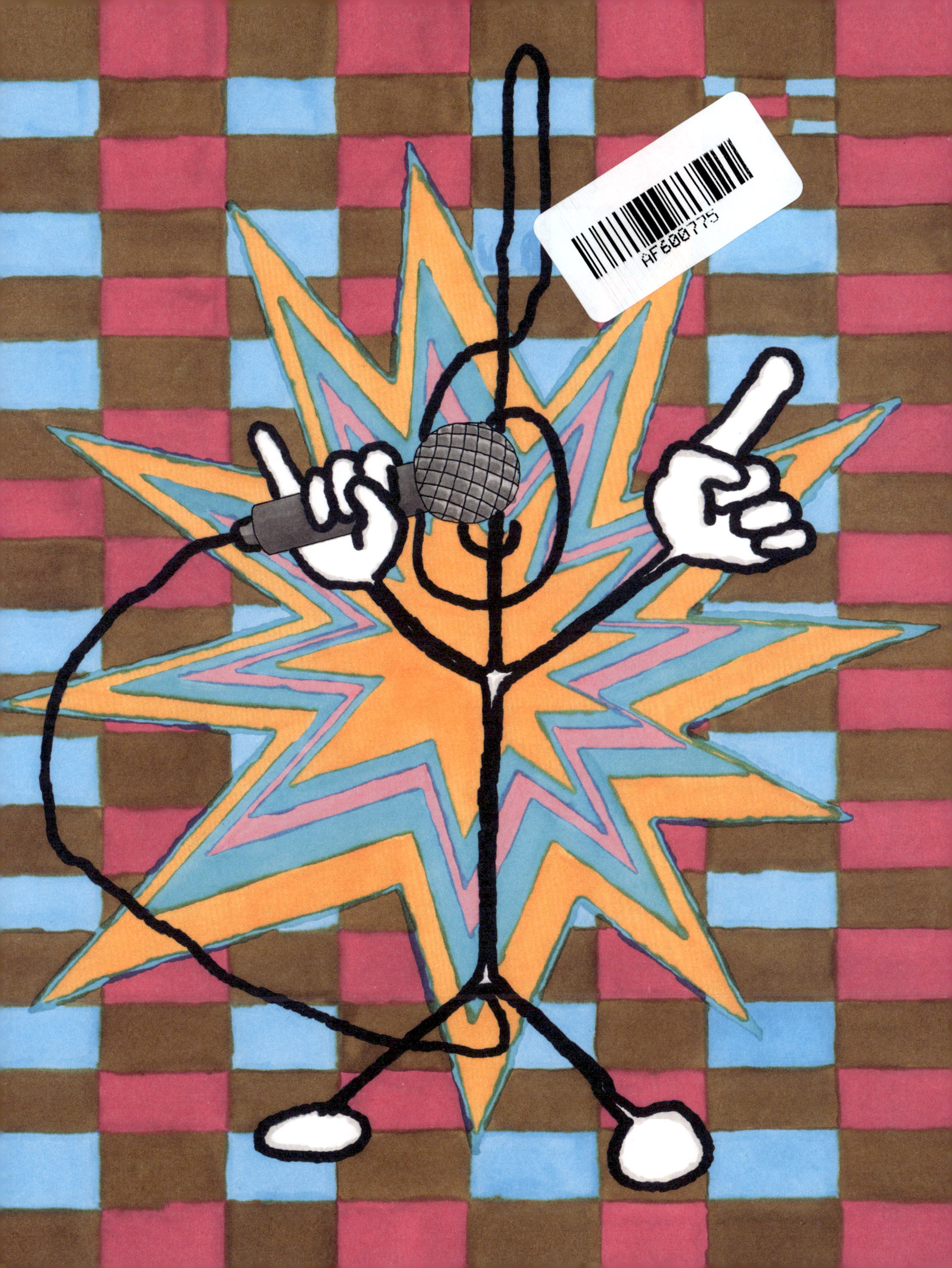

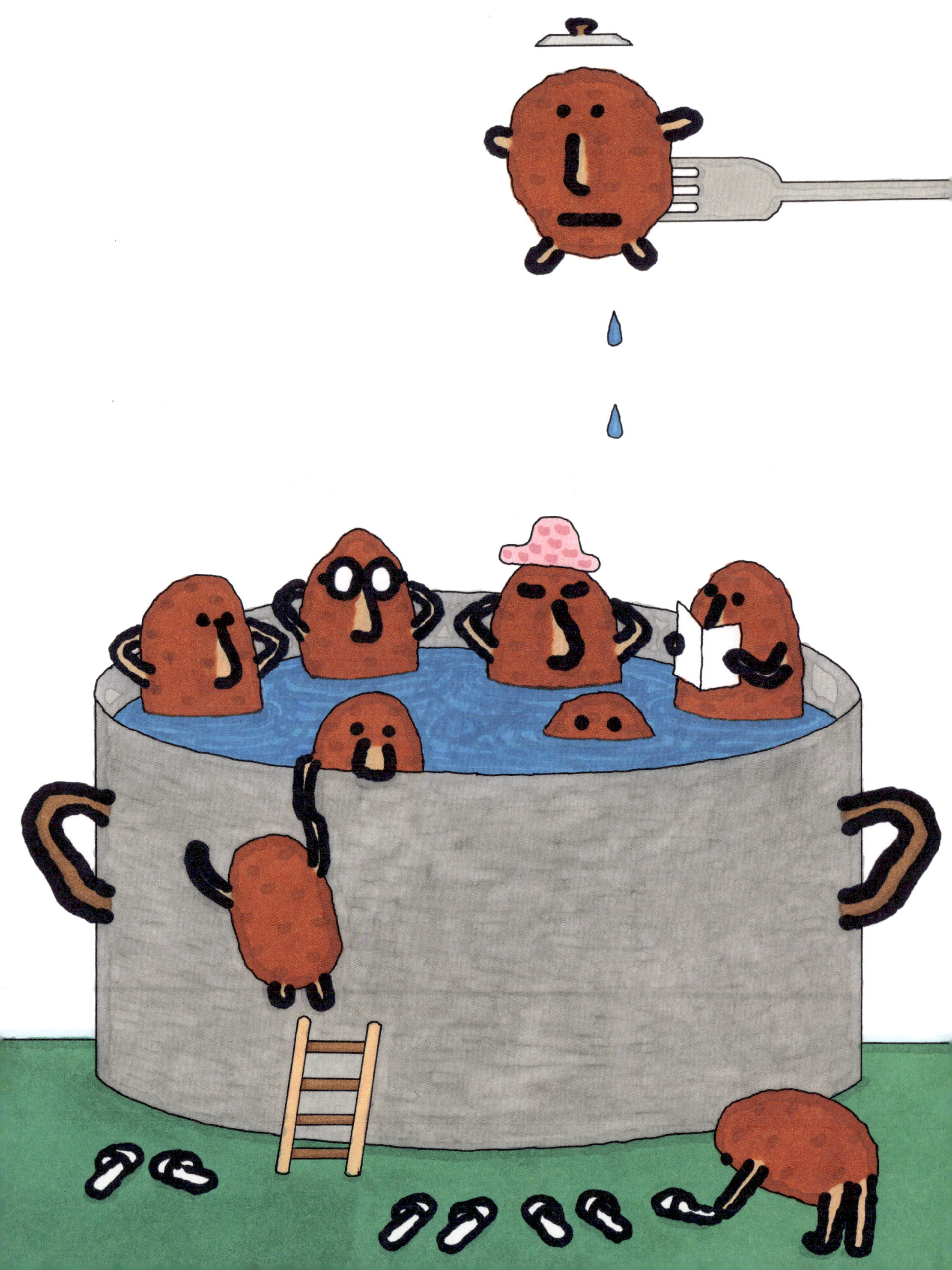

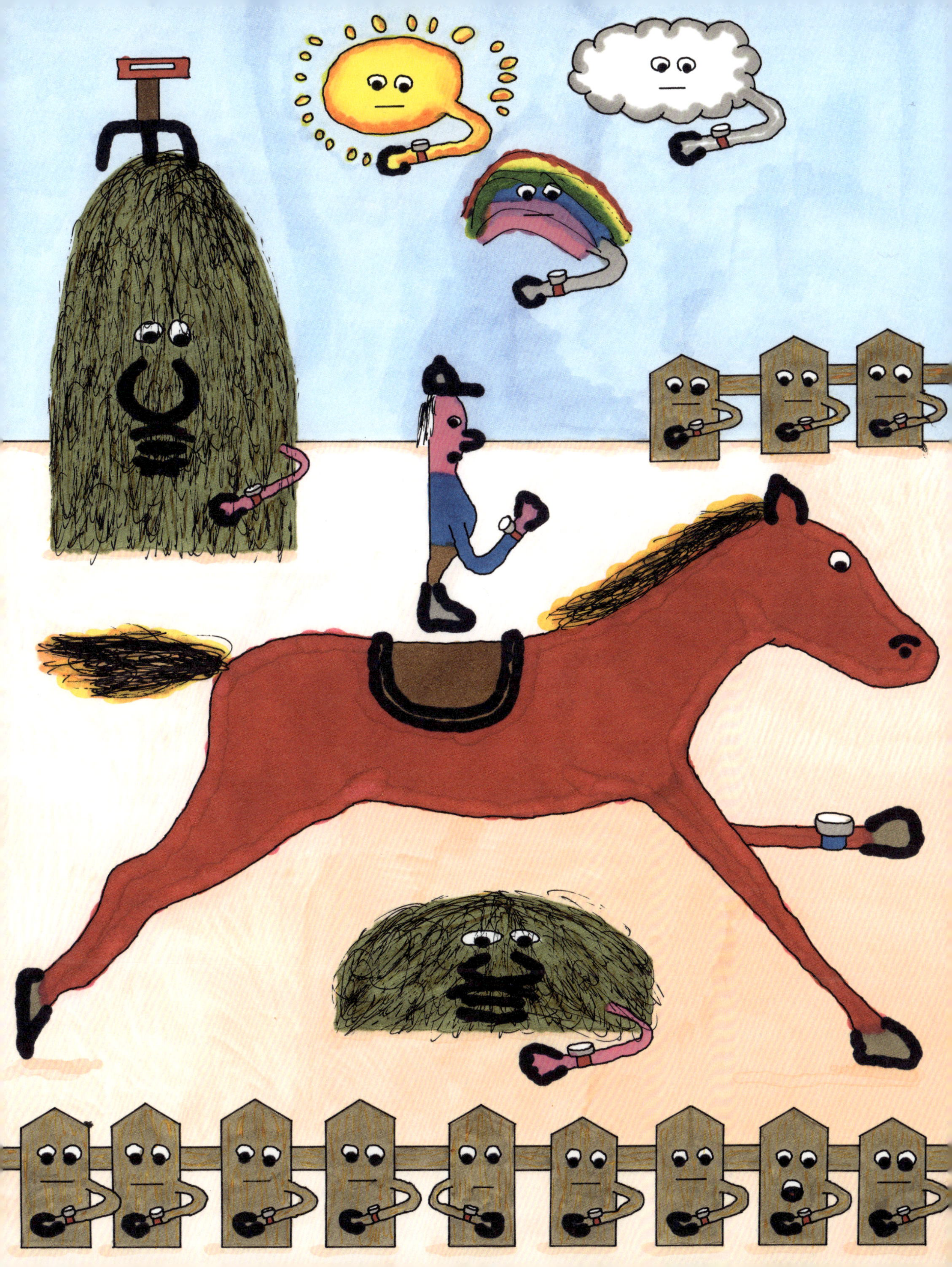

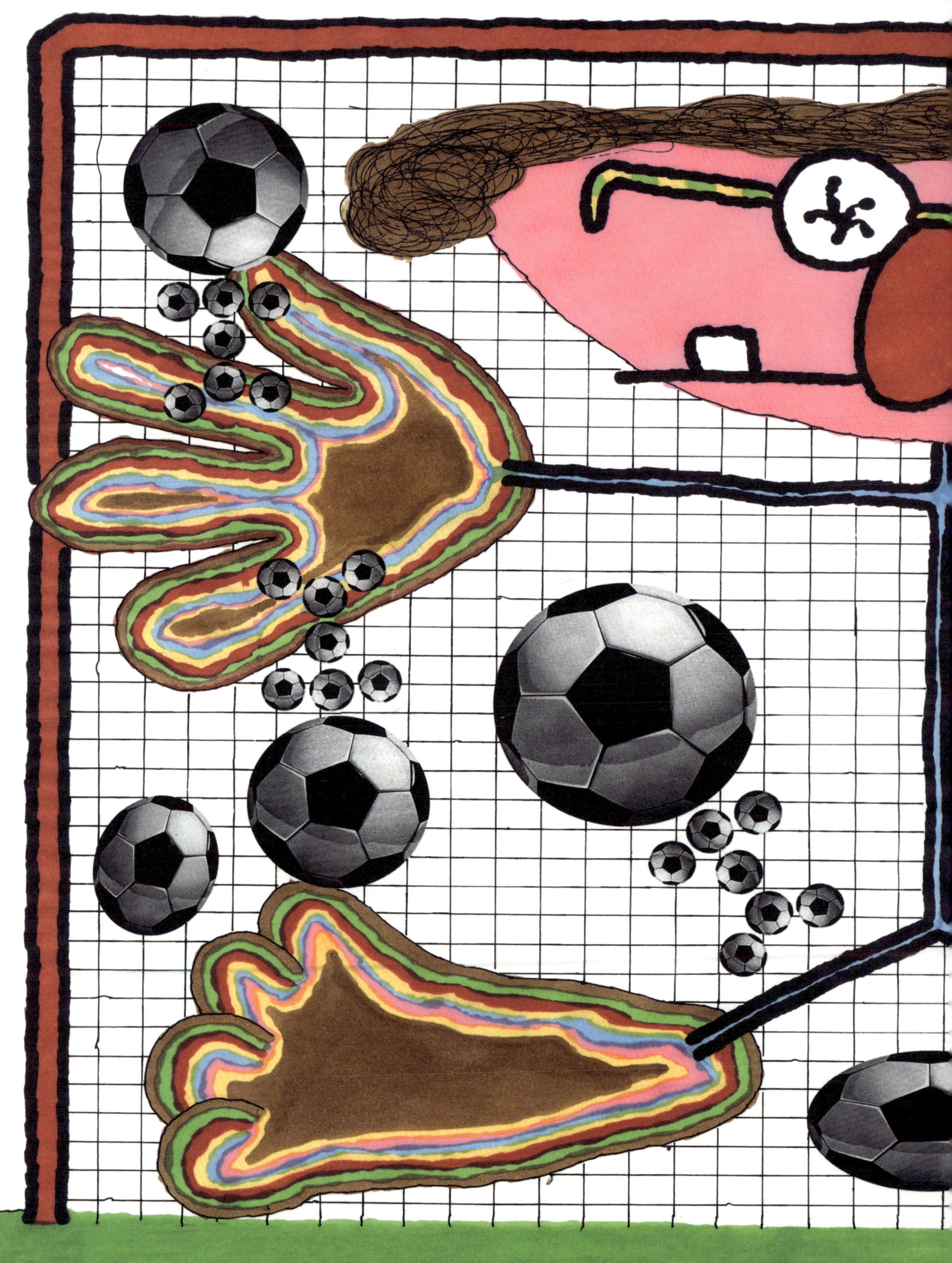

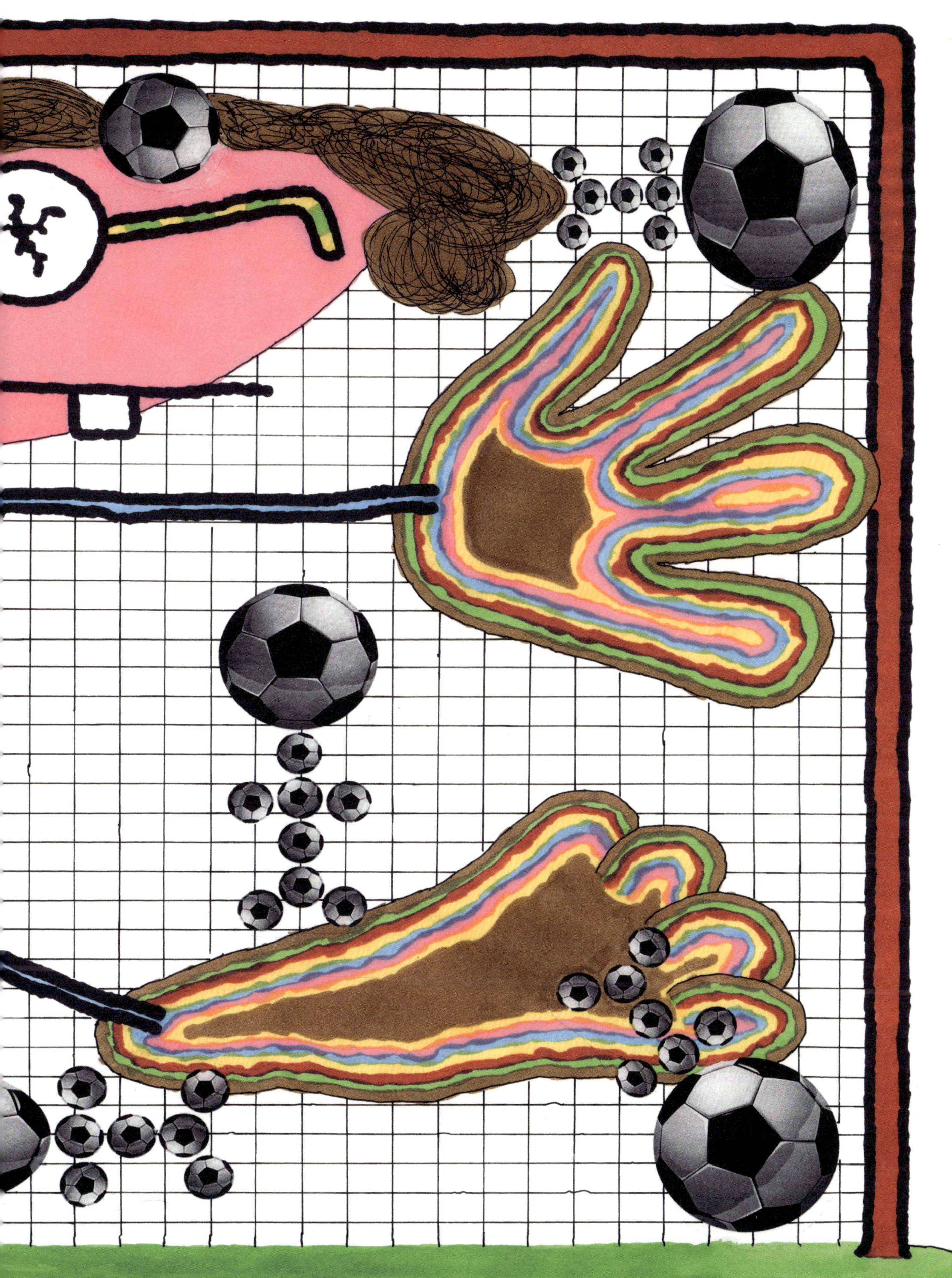

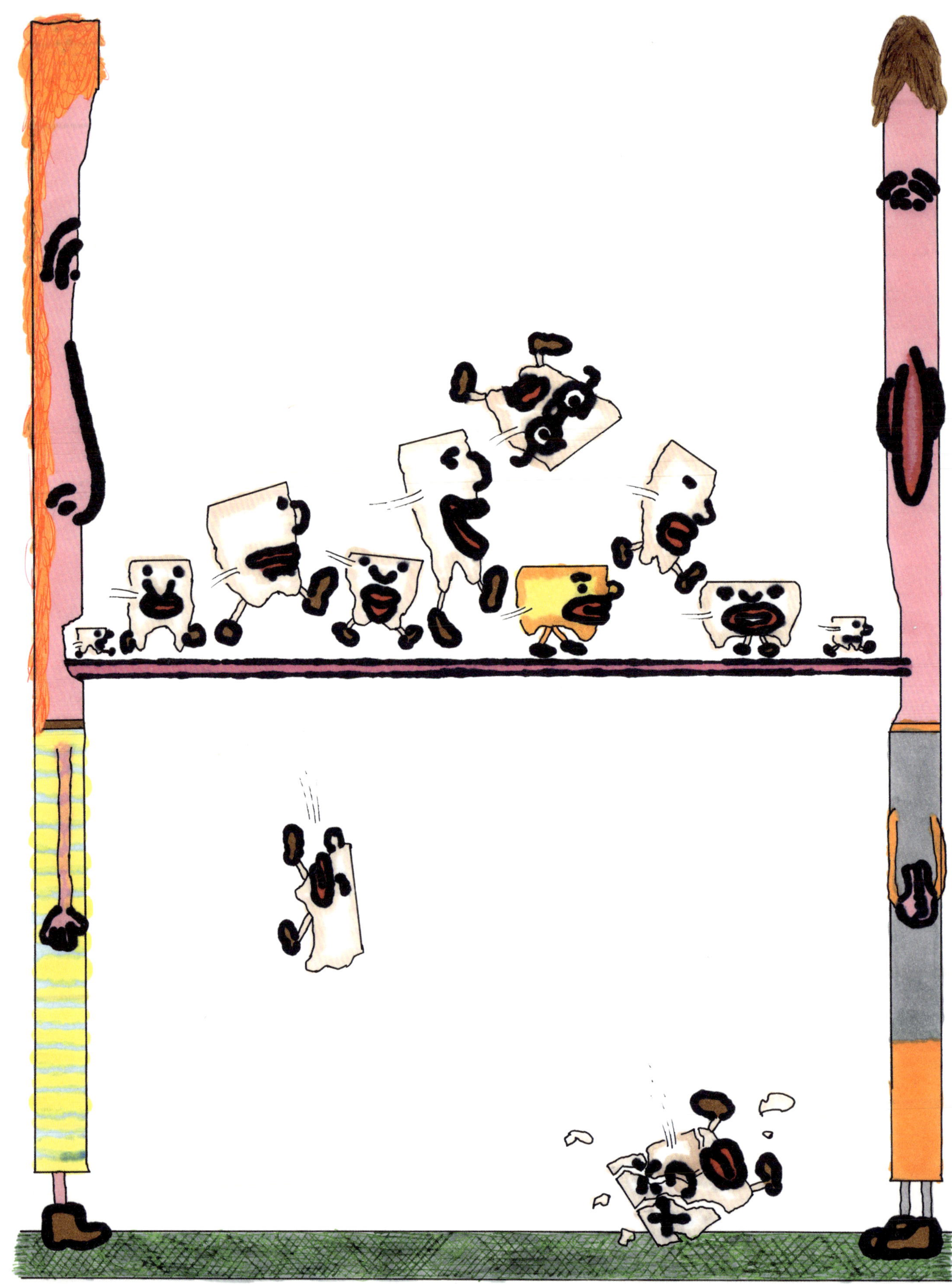

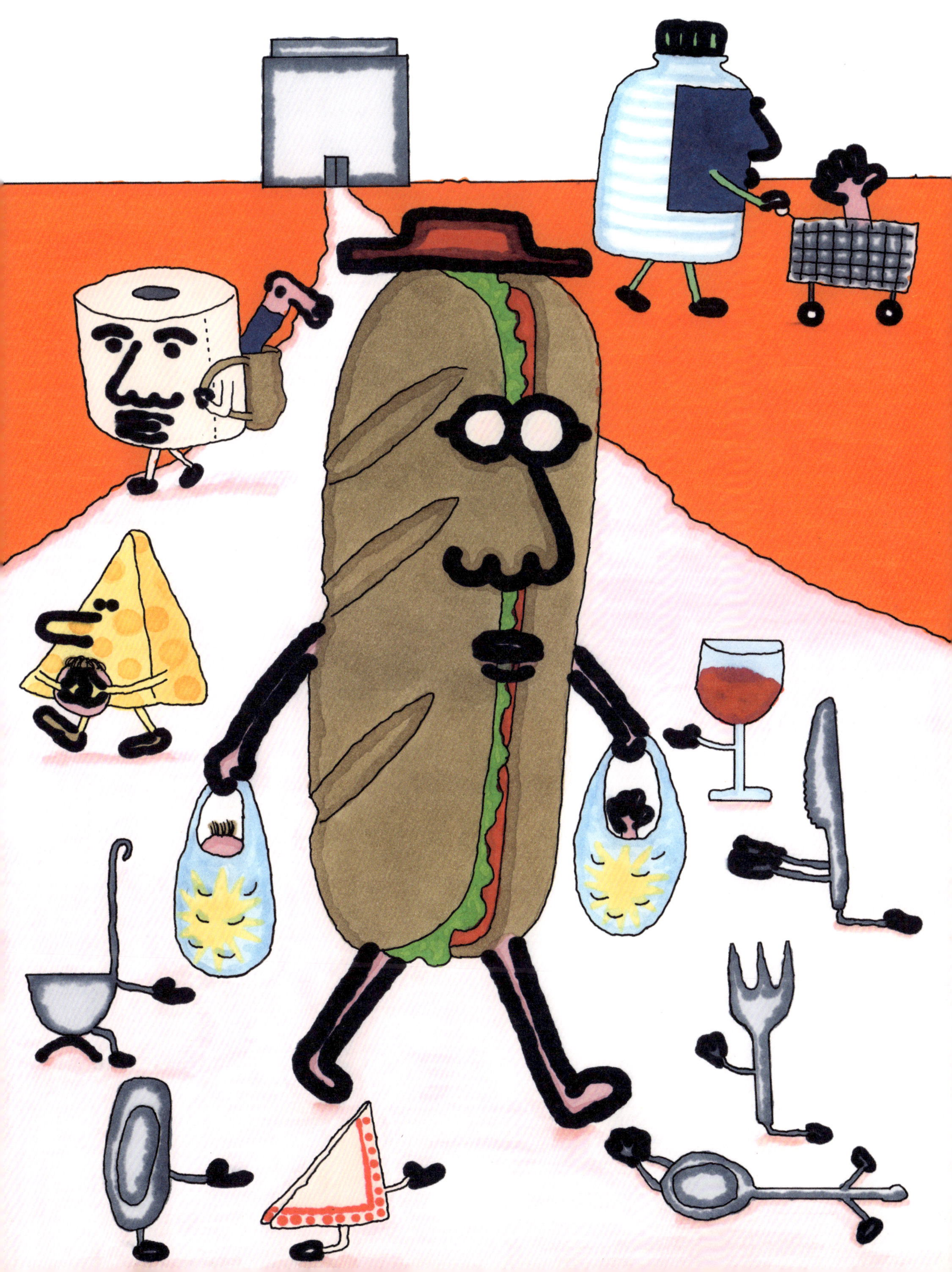

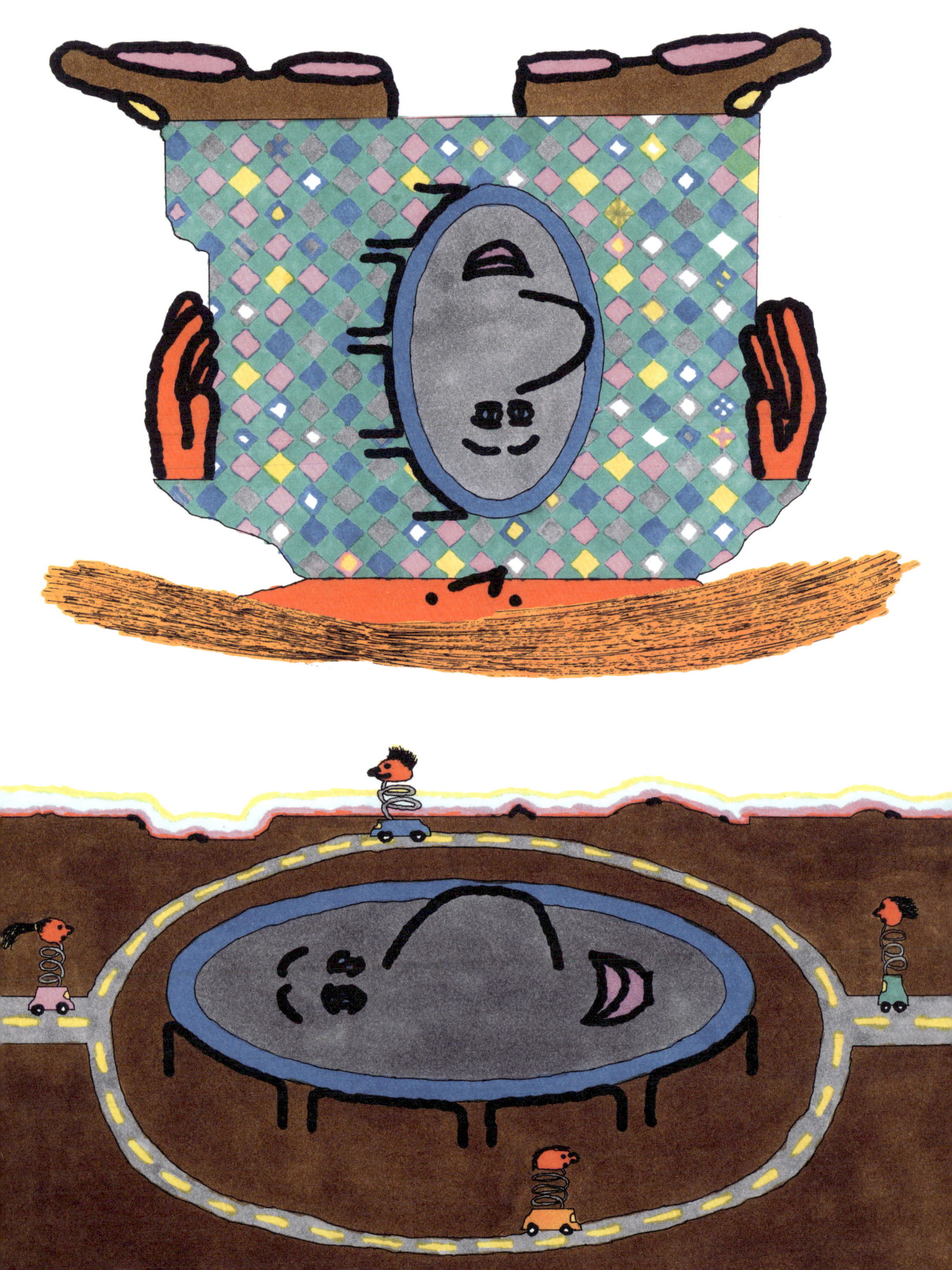

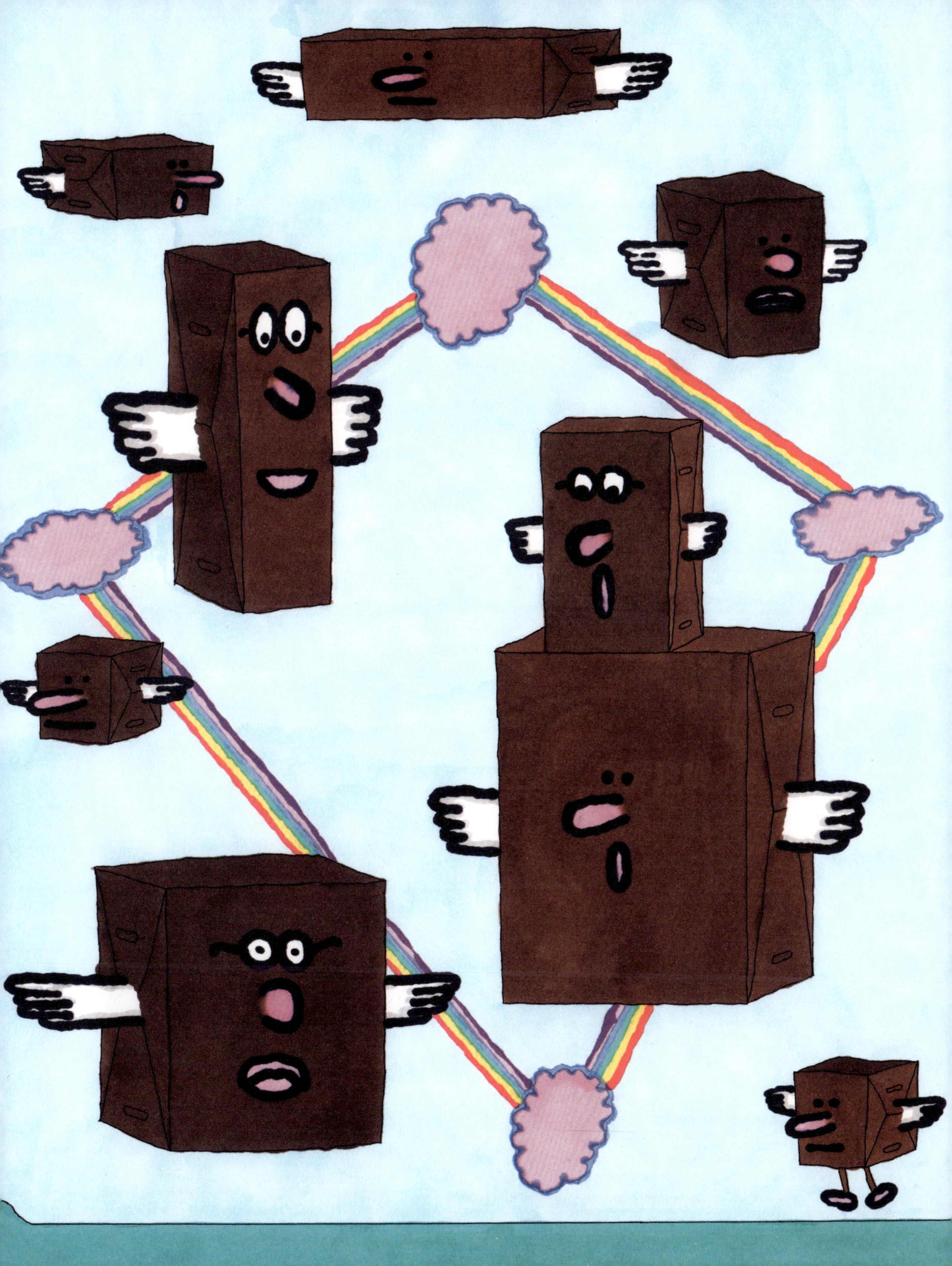

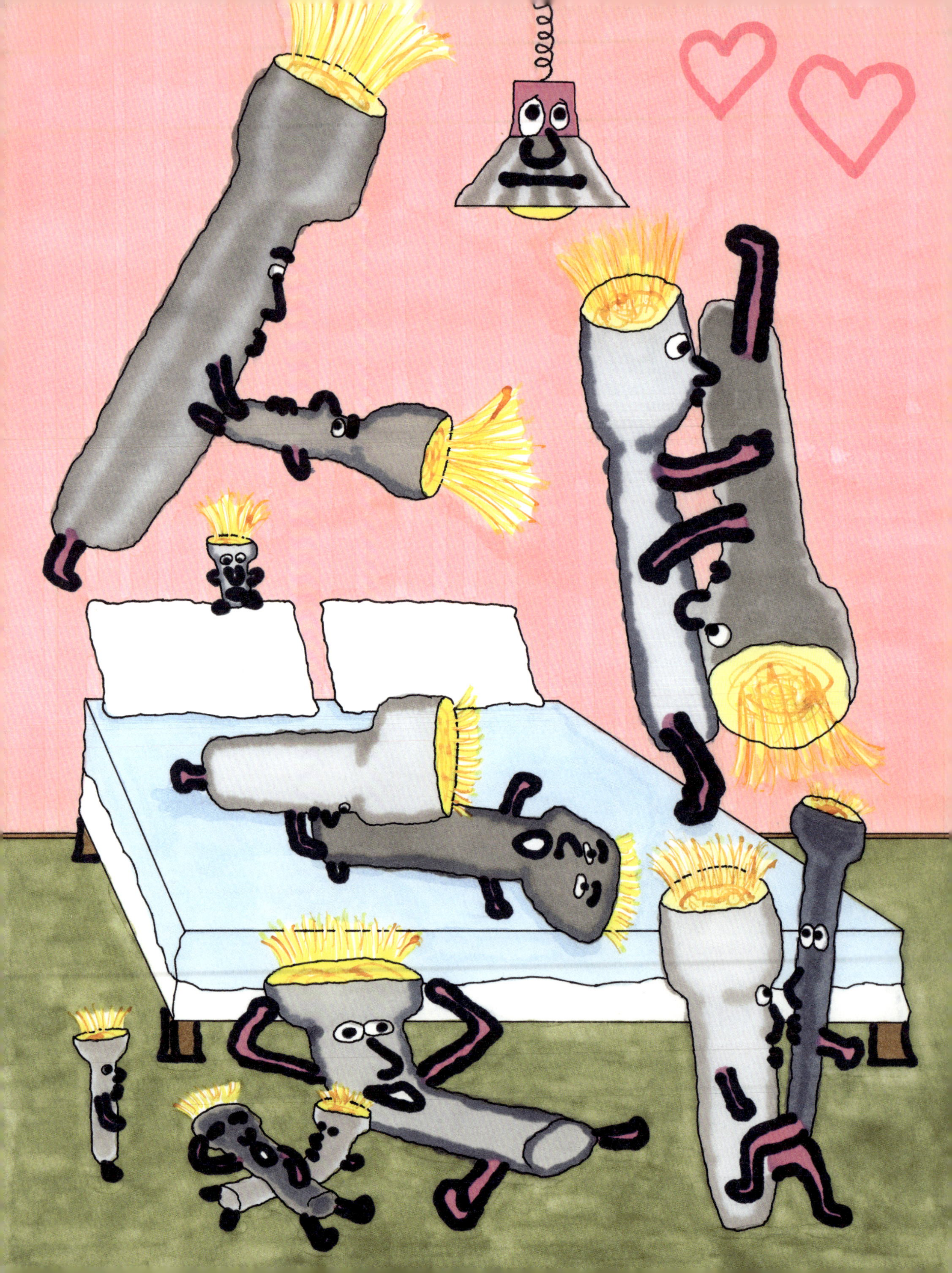

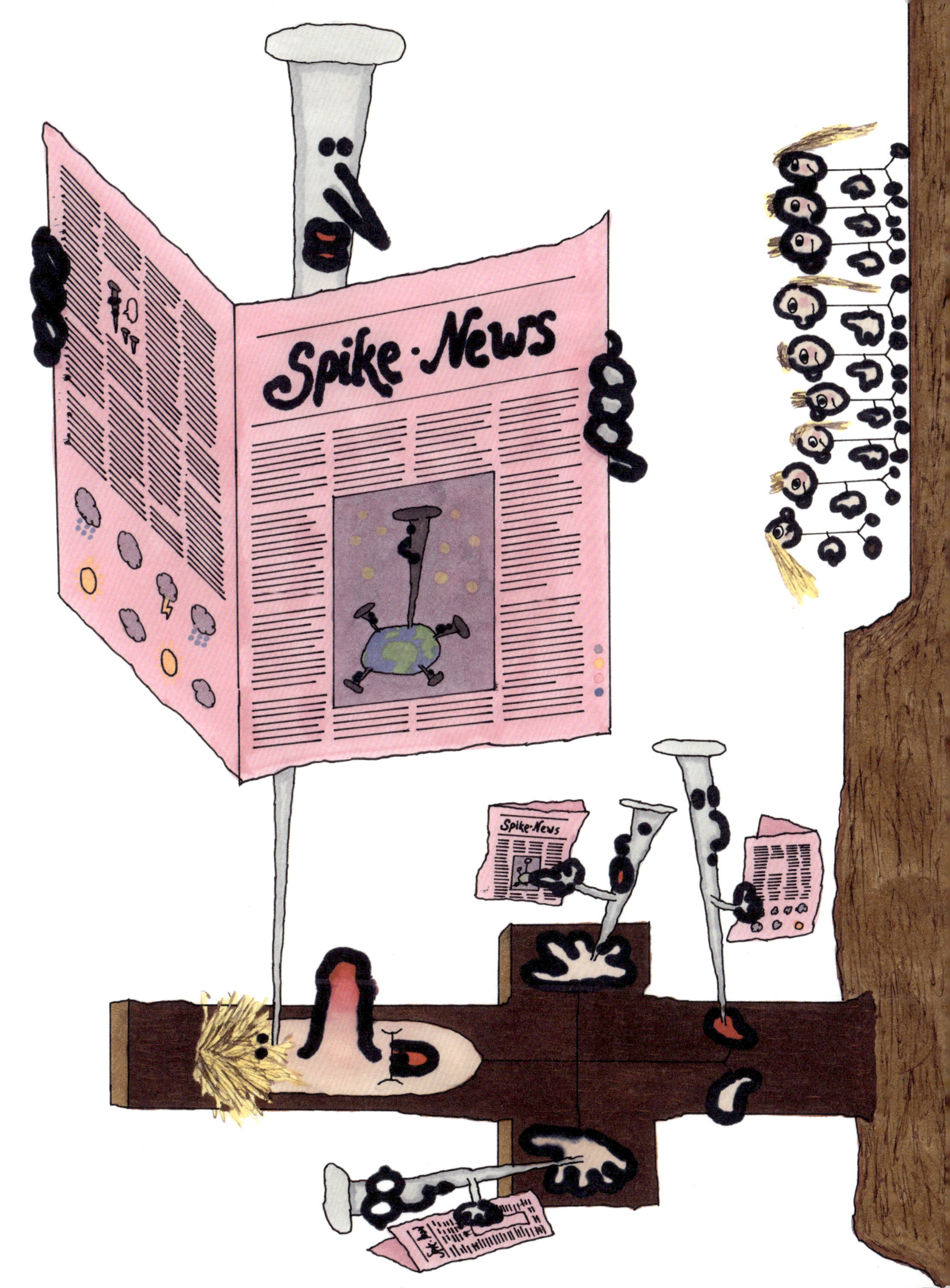
Spike·News
Spike-News

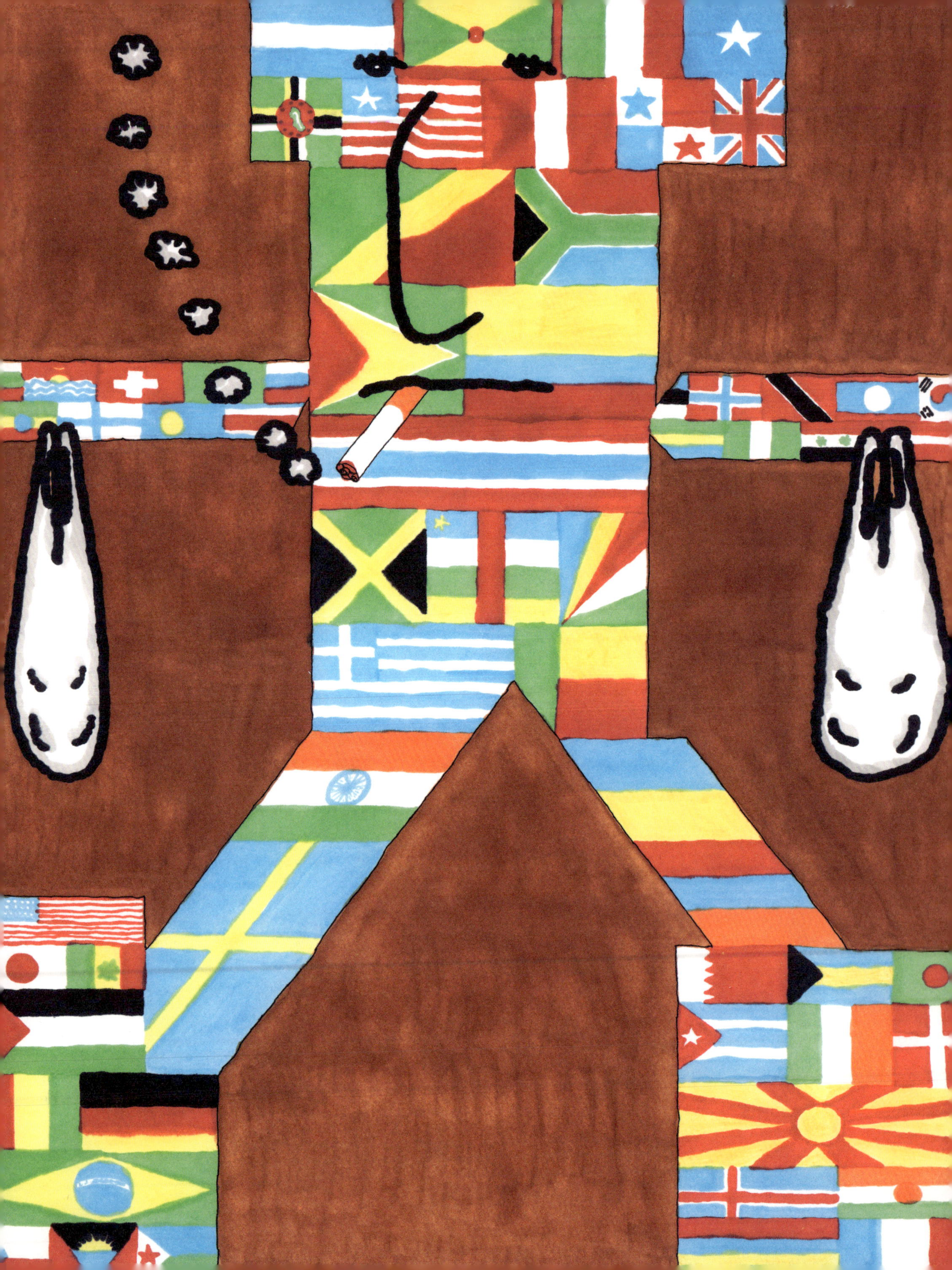

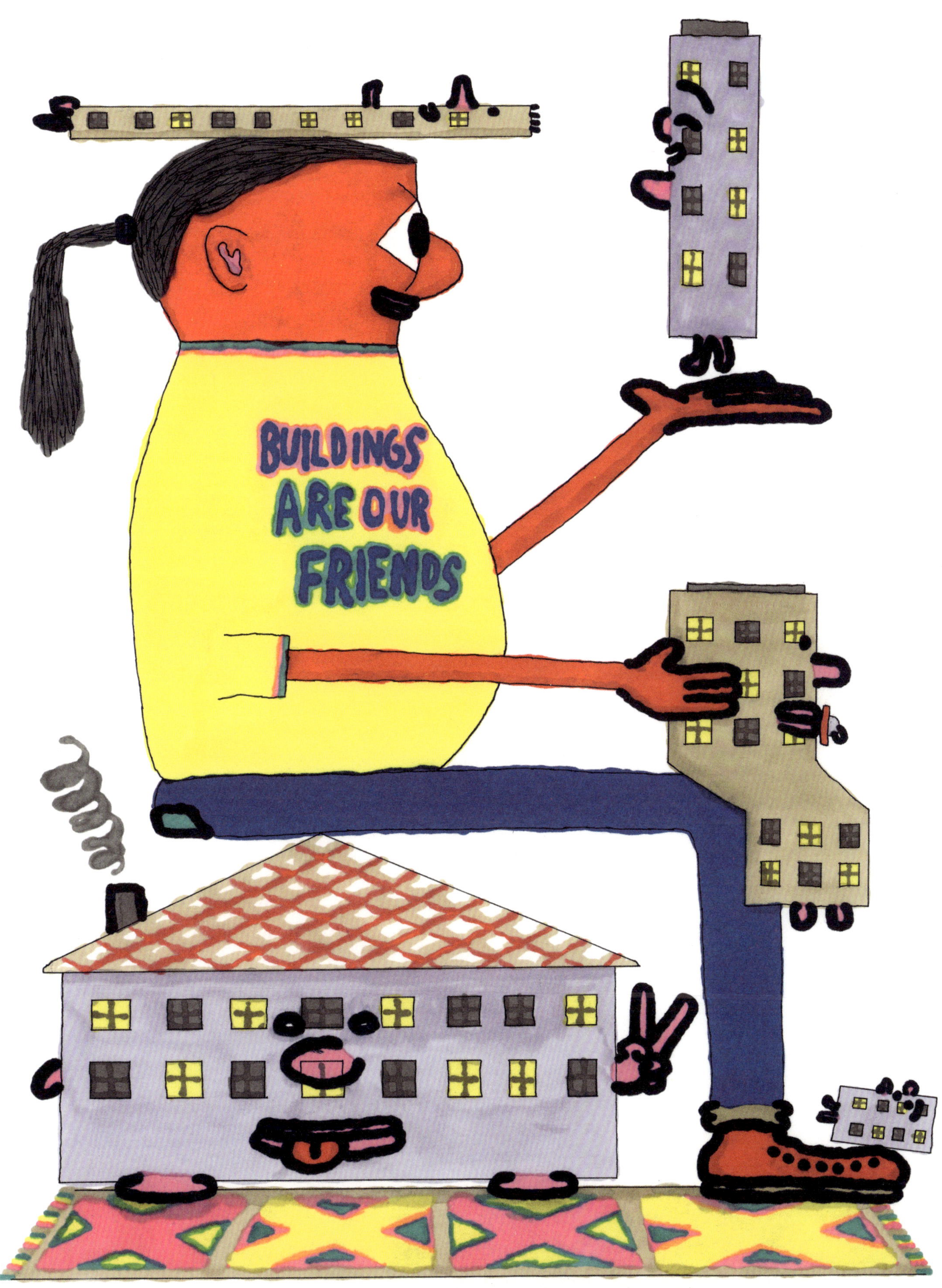
BUILDINGS ARE OUR FRIENDS

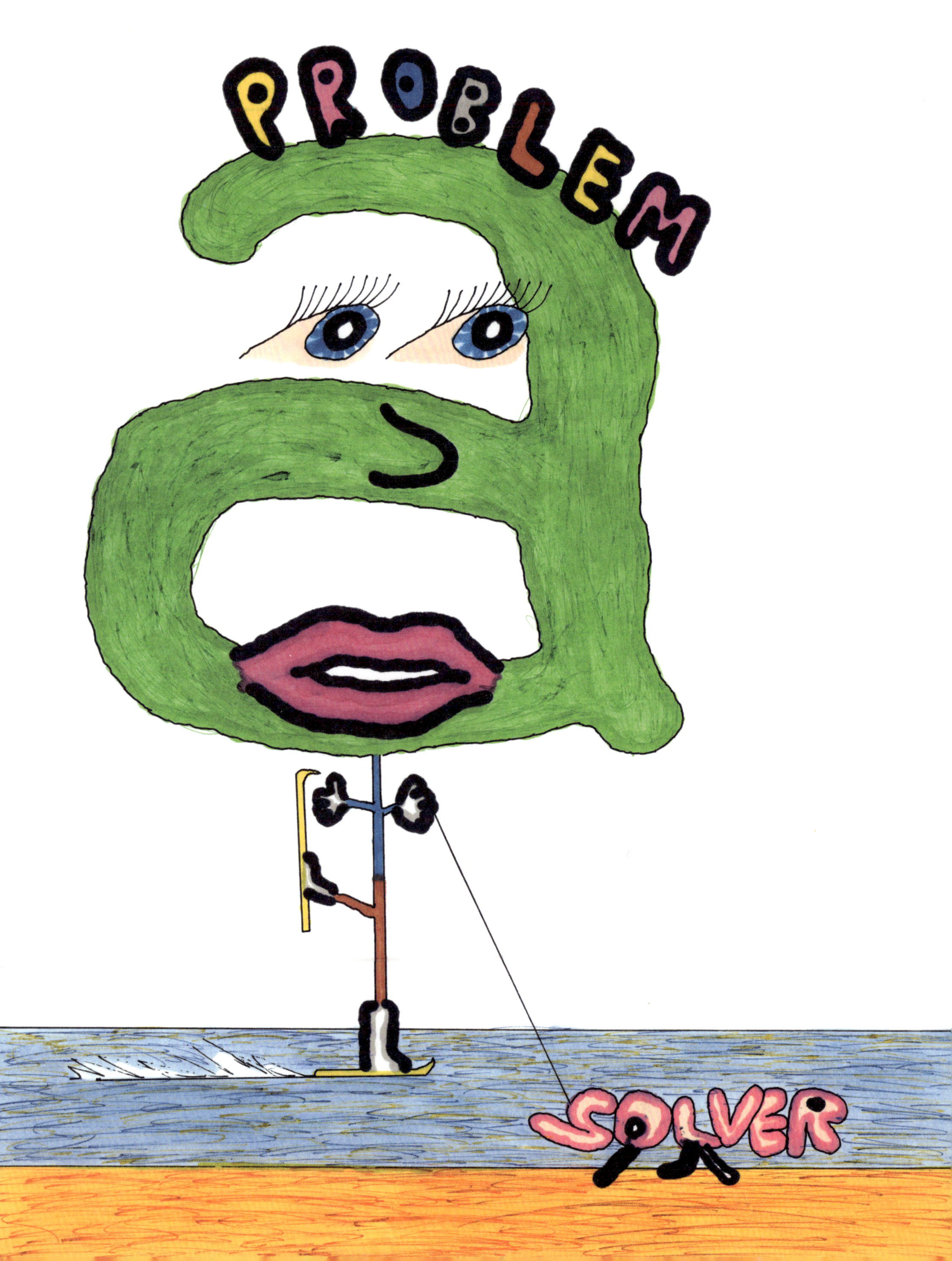
PROBLEM
SOLVER

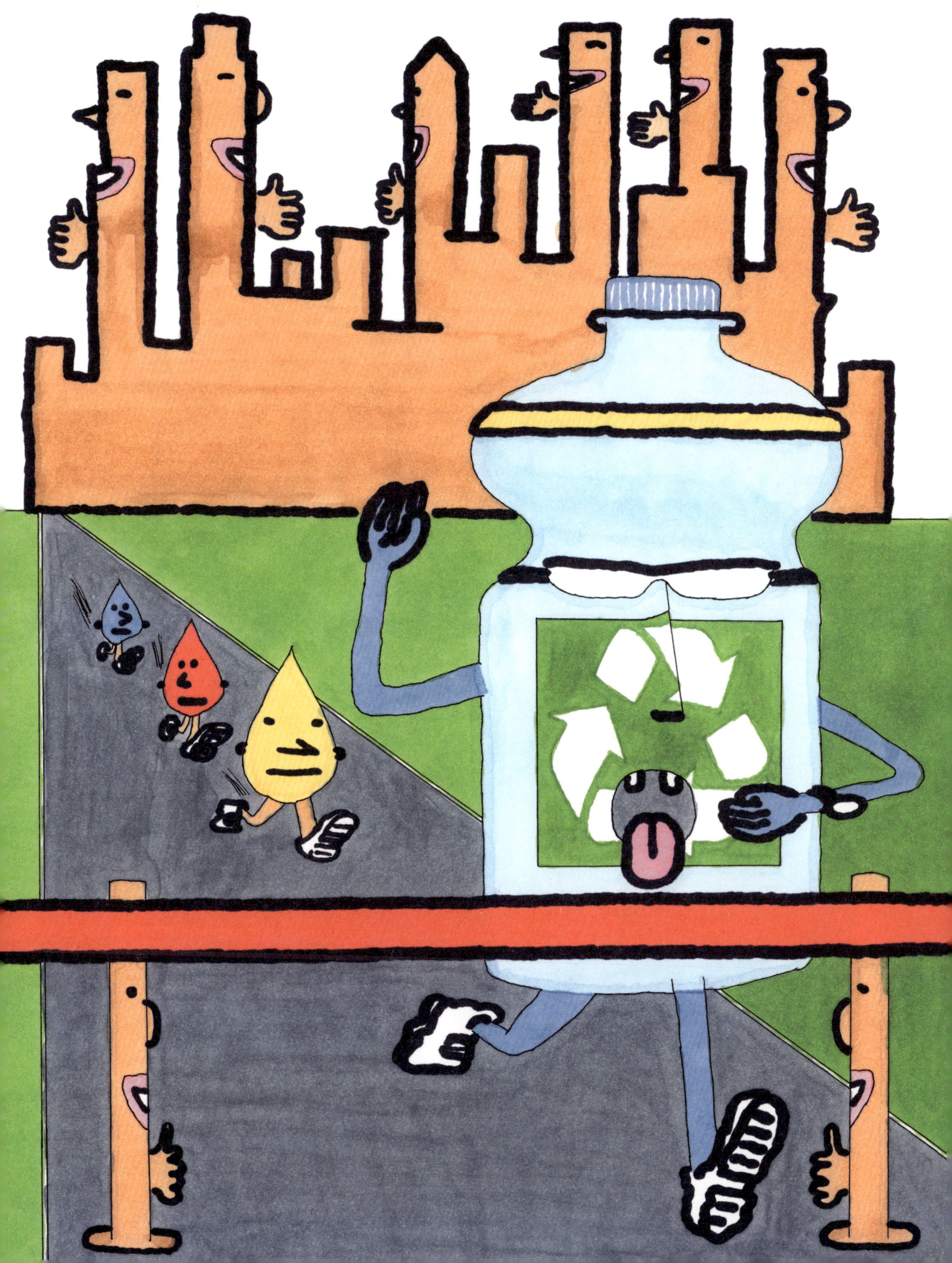

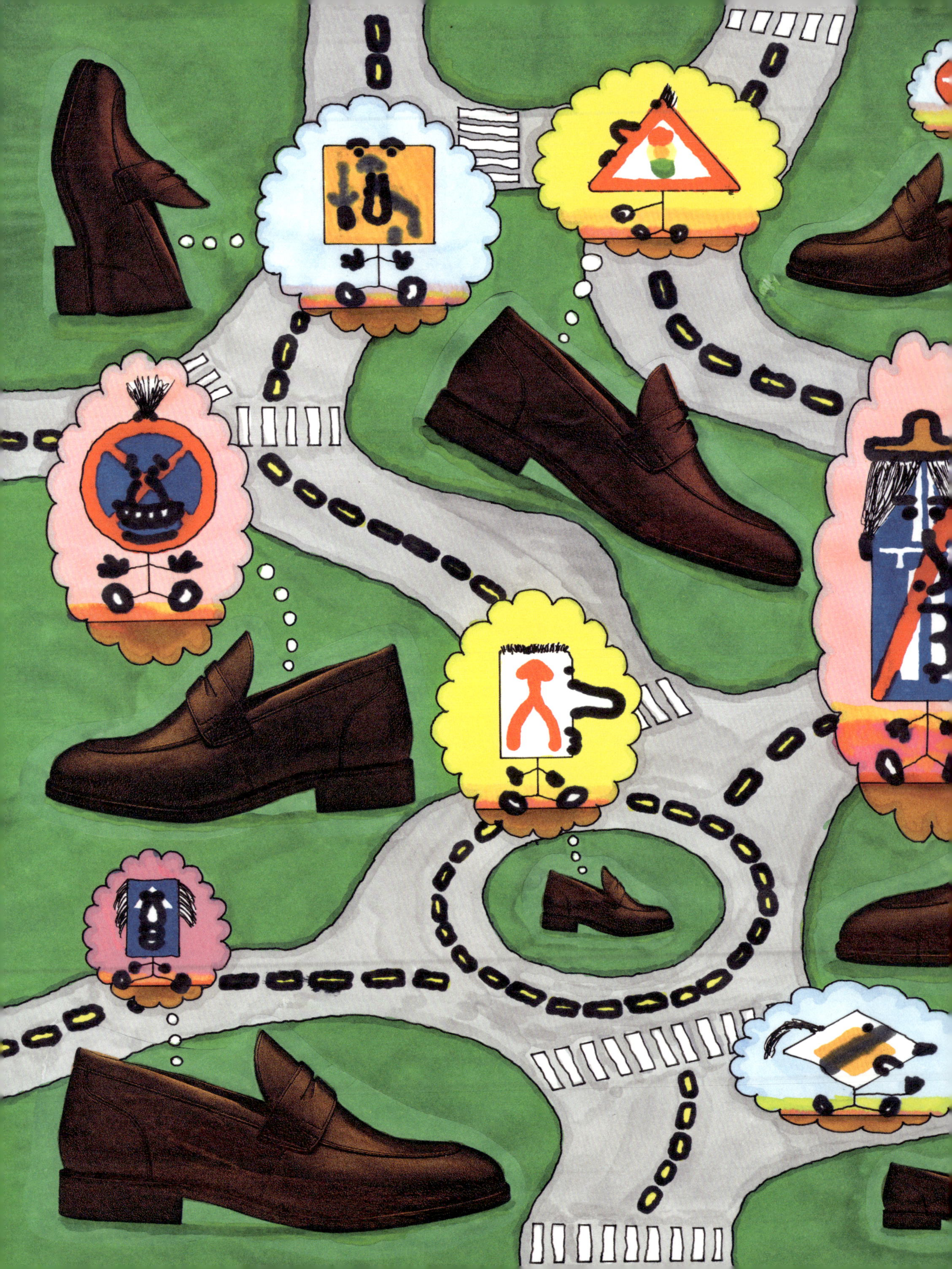

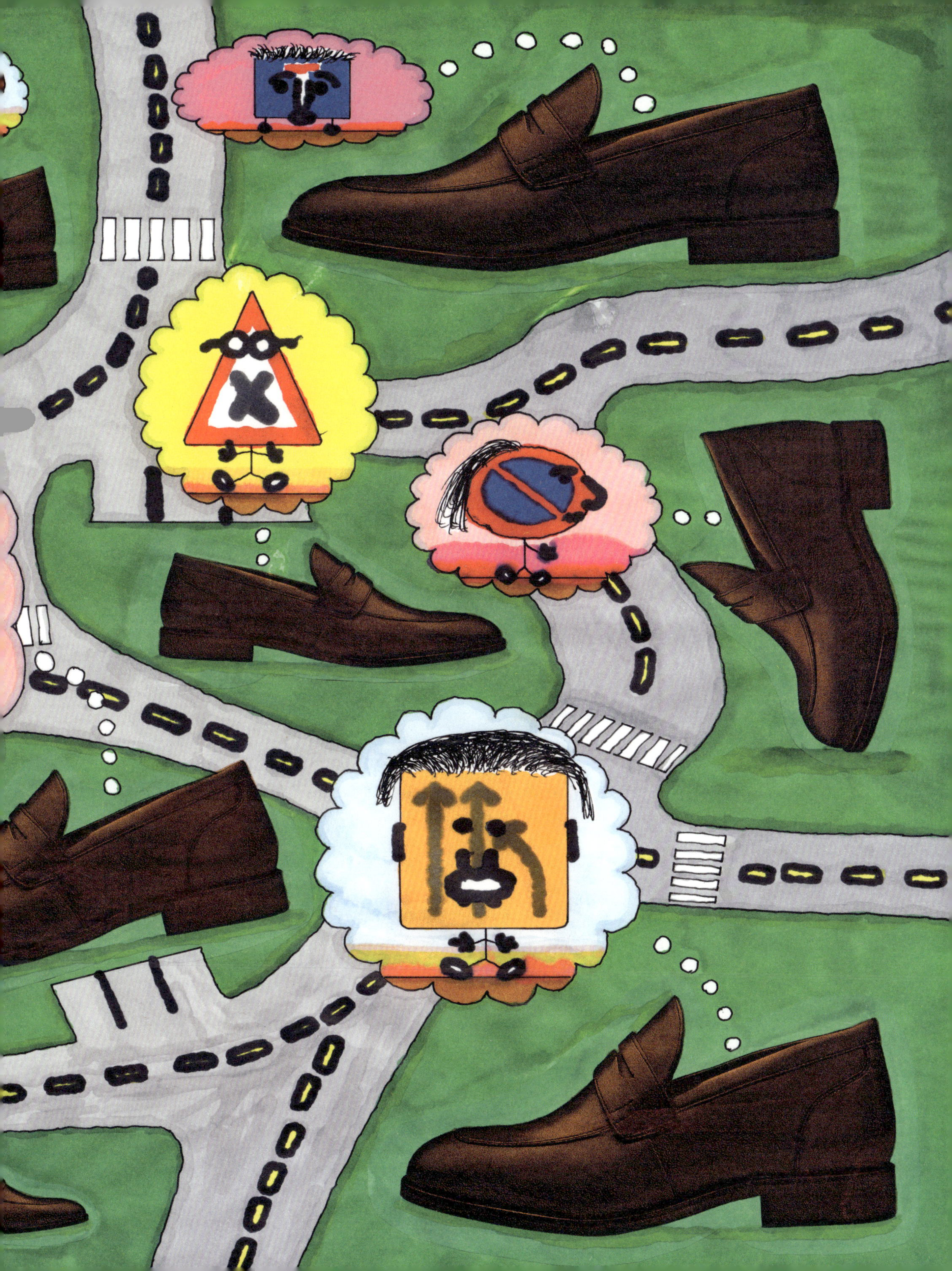

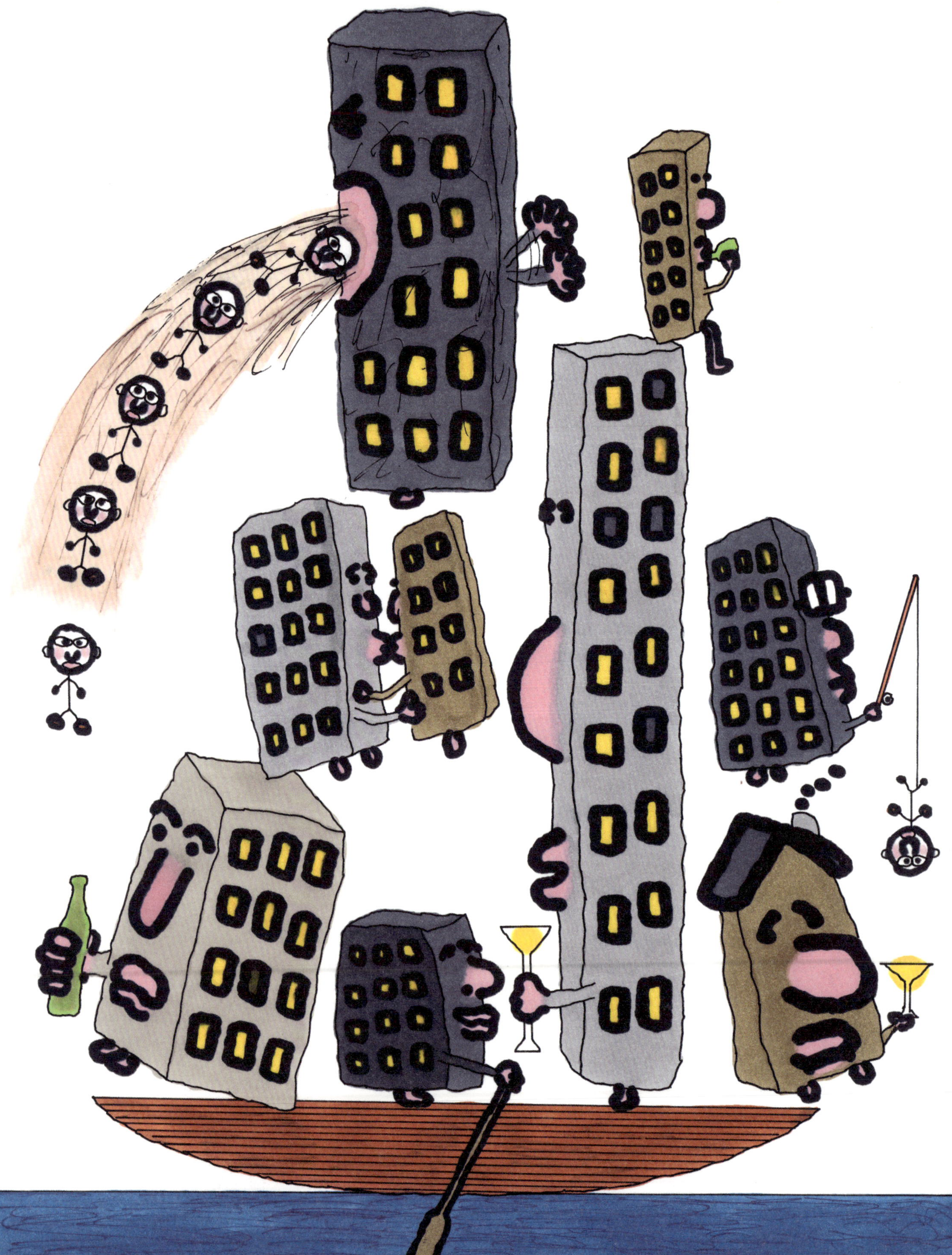

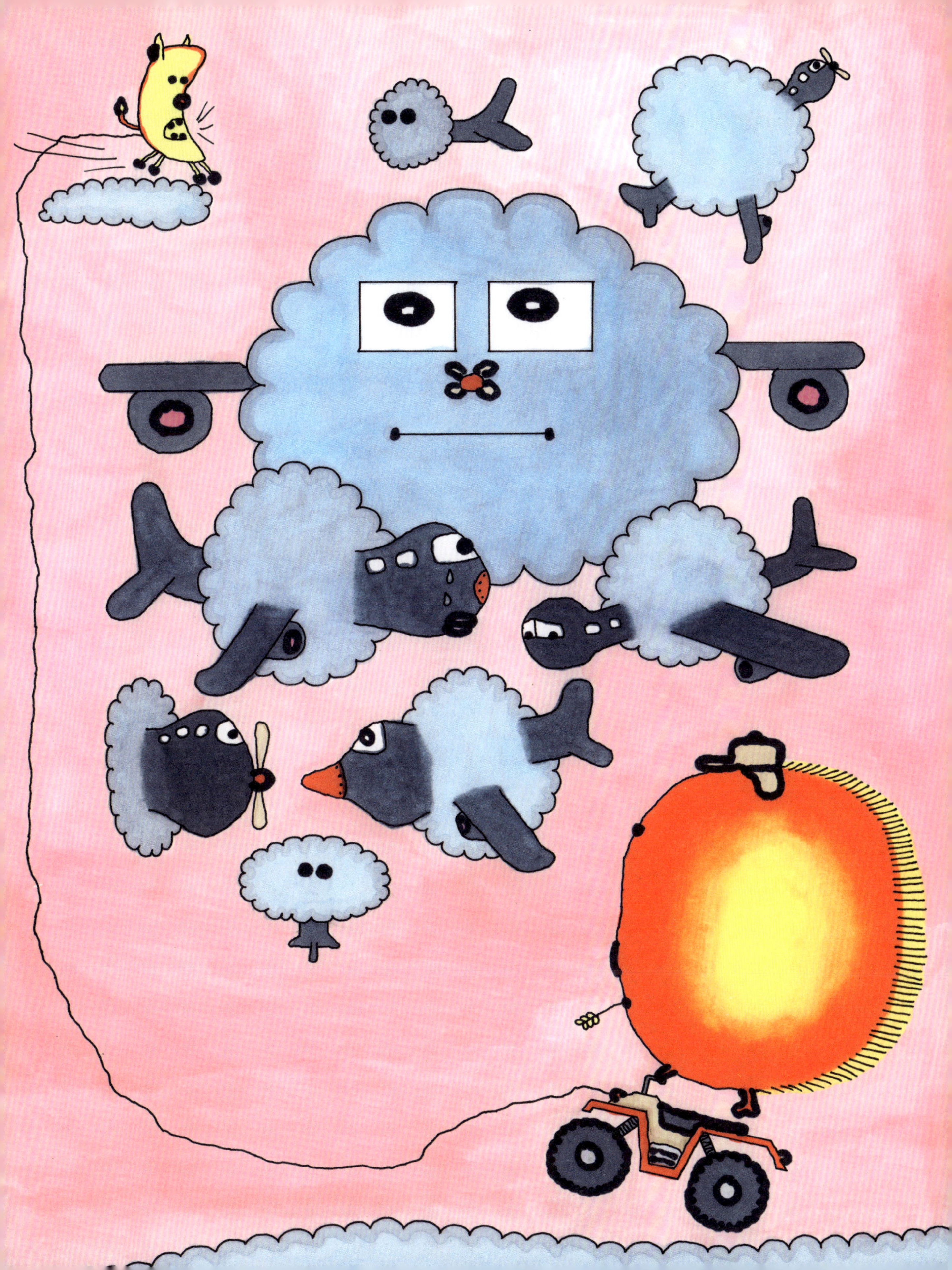

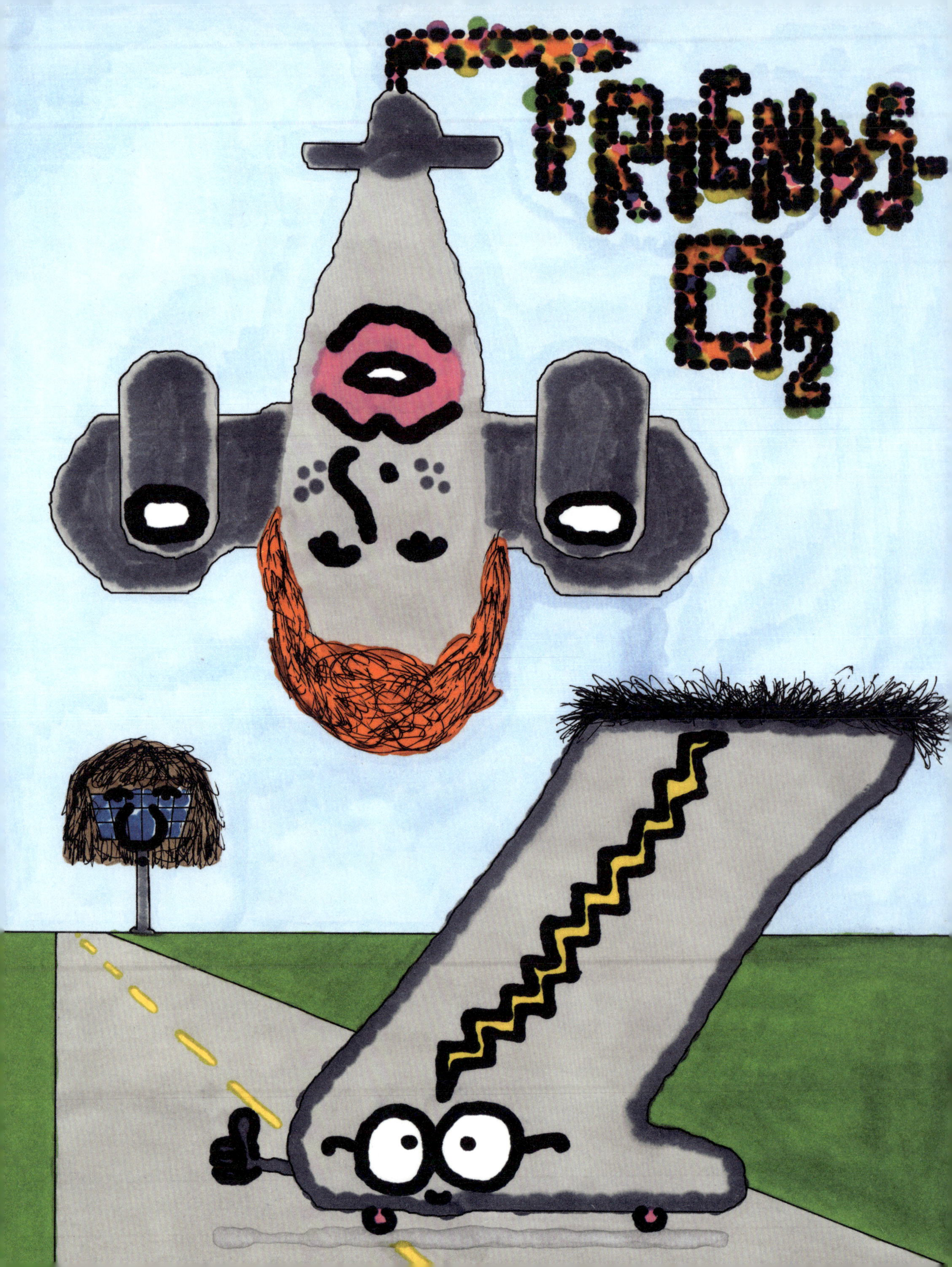

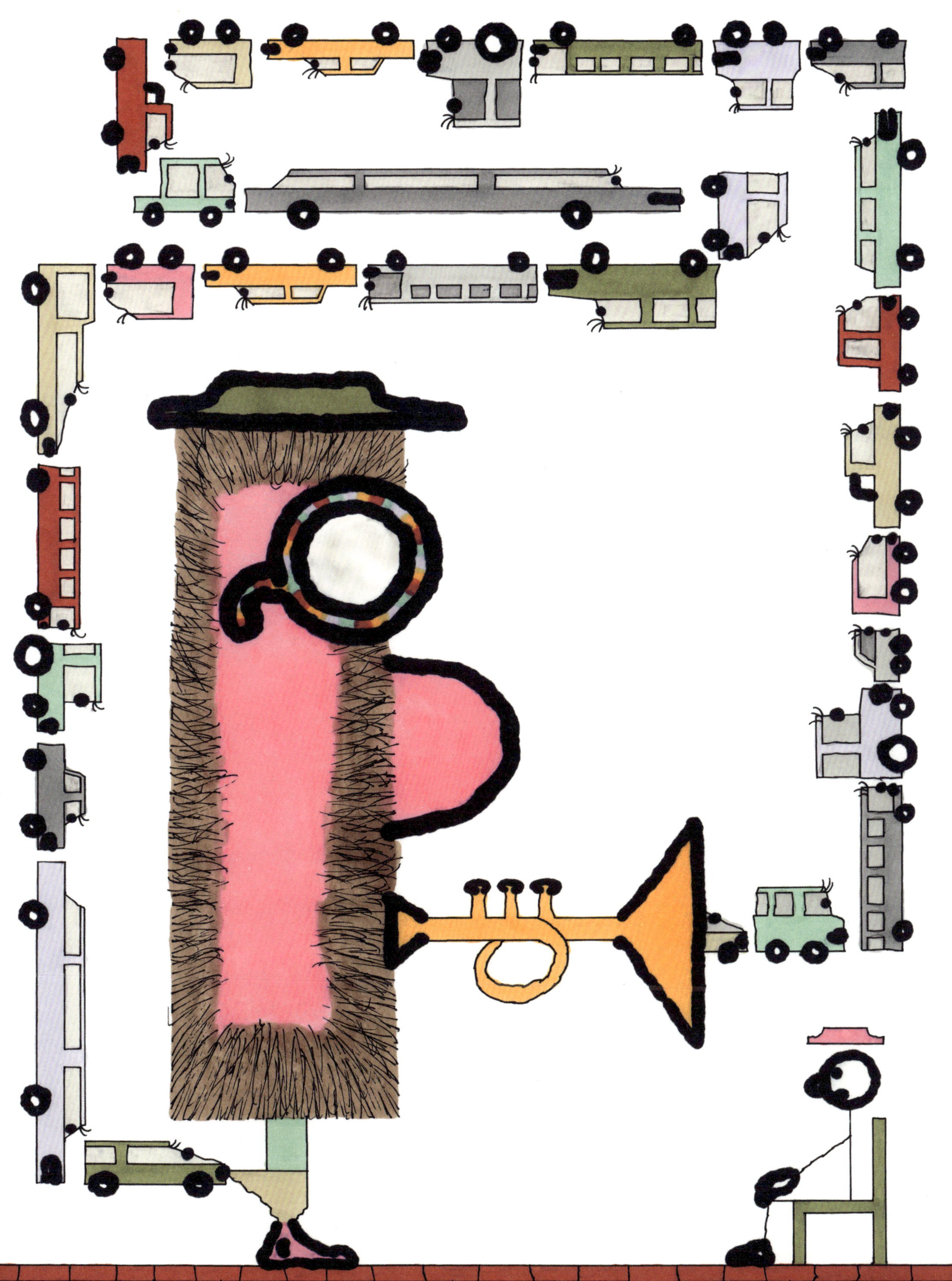

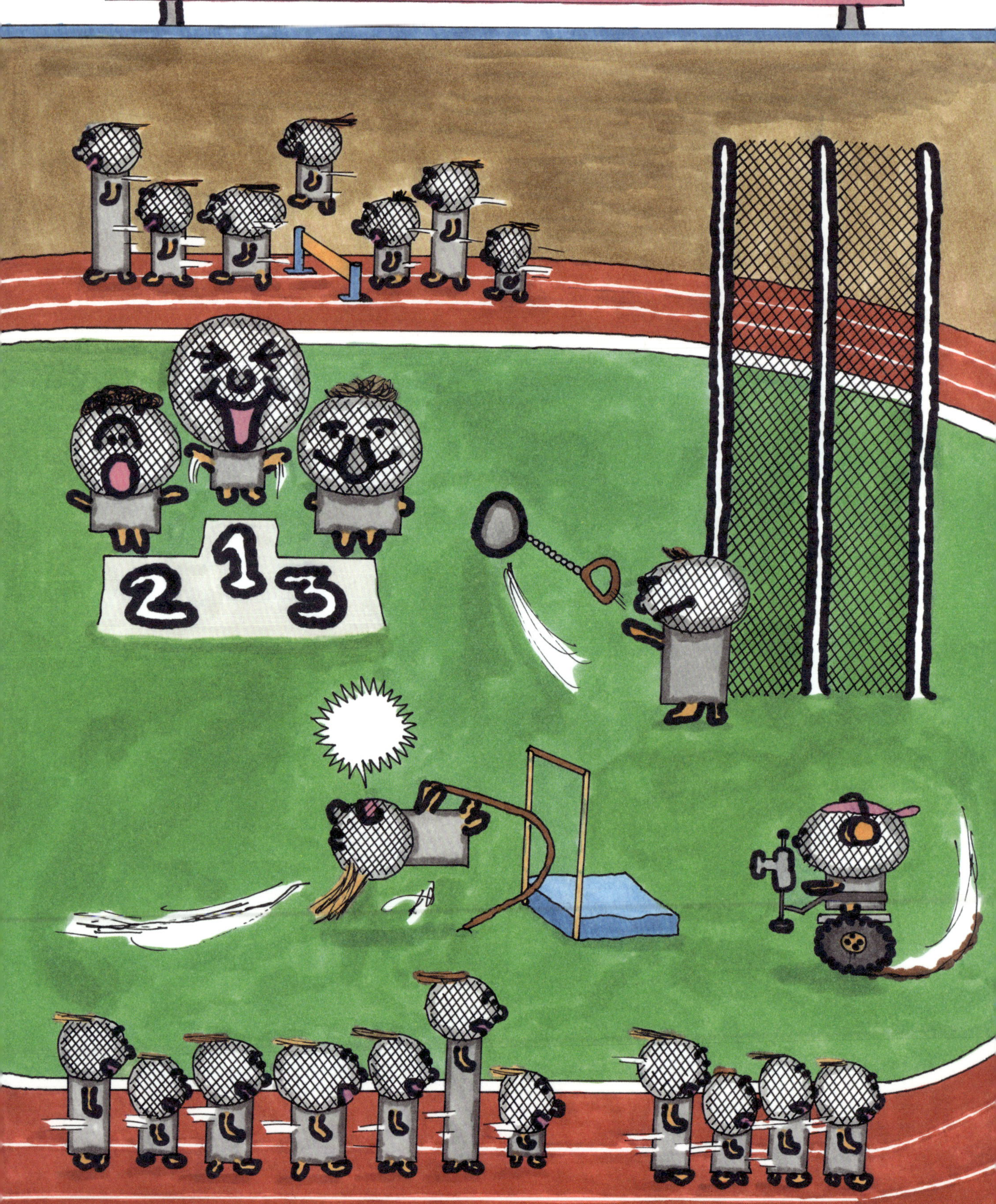
WIRELESS MICROPHONE OLYMPICS
2 1 3

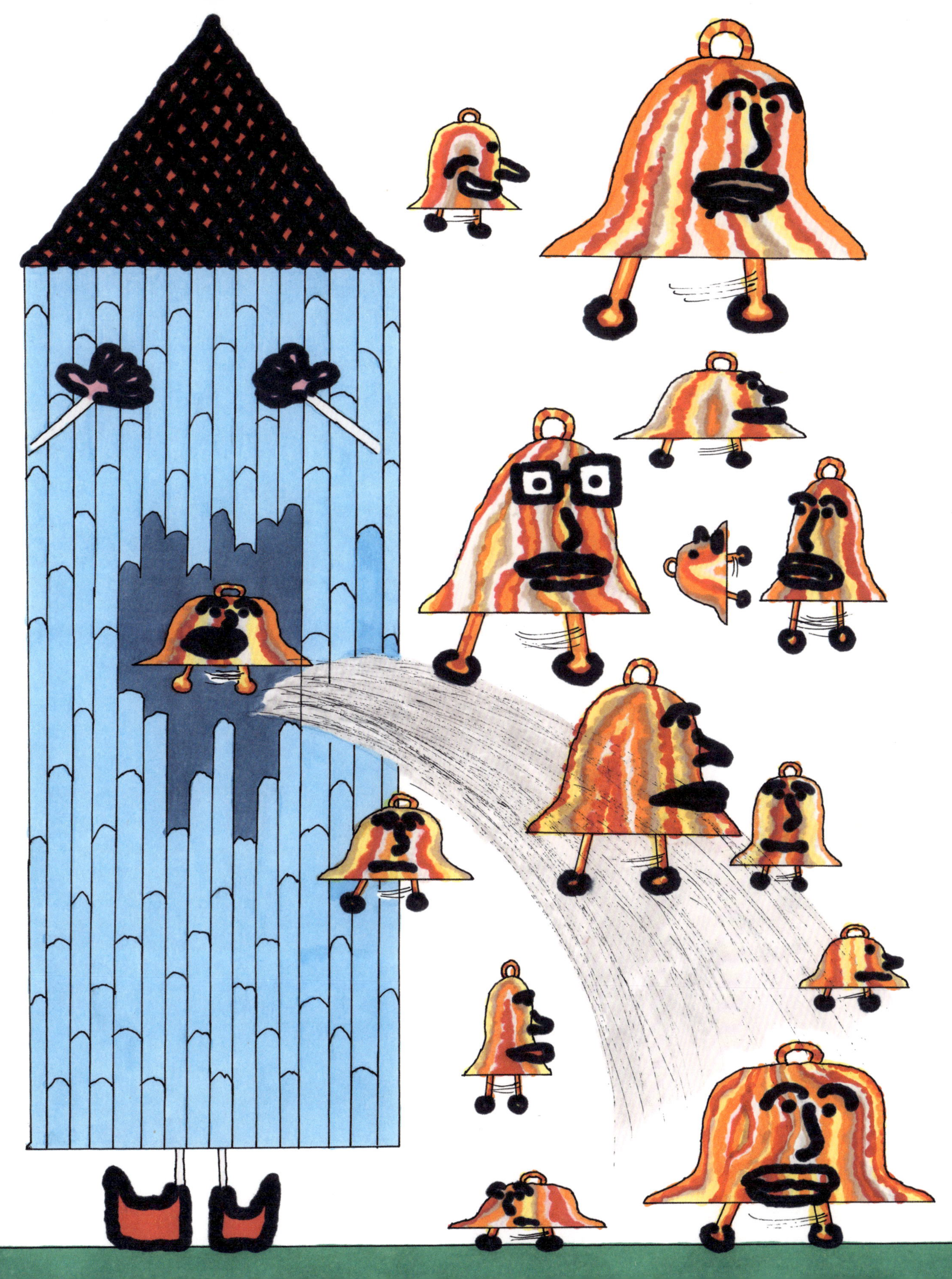

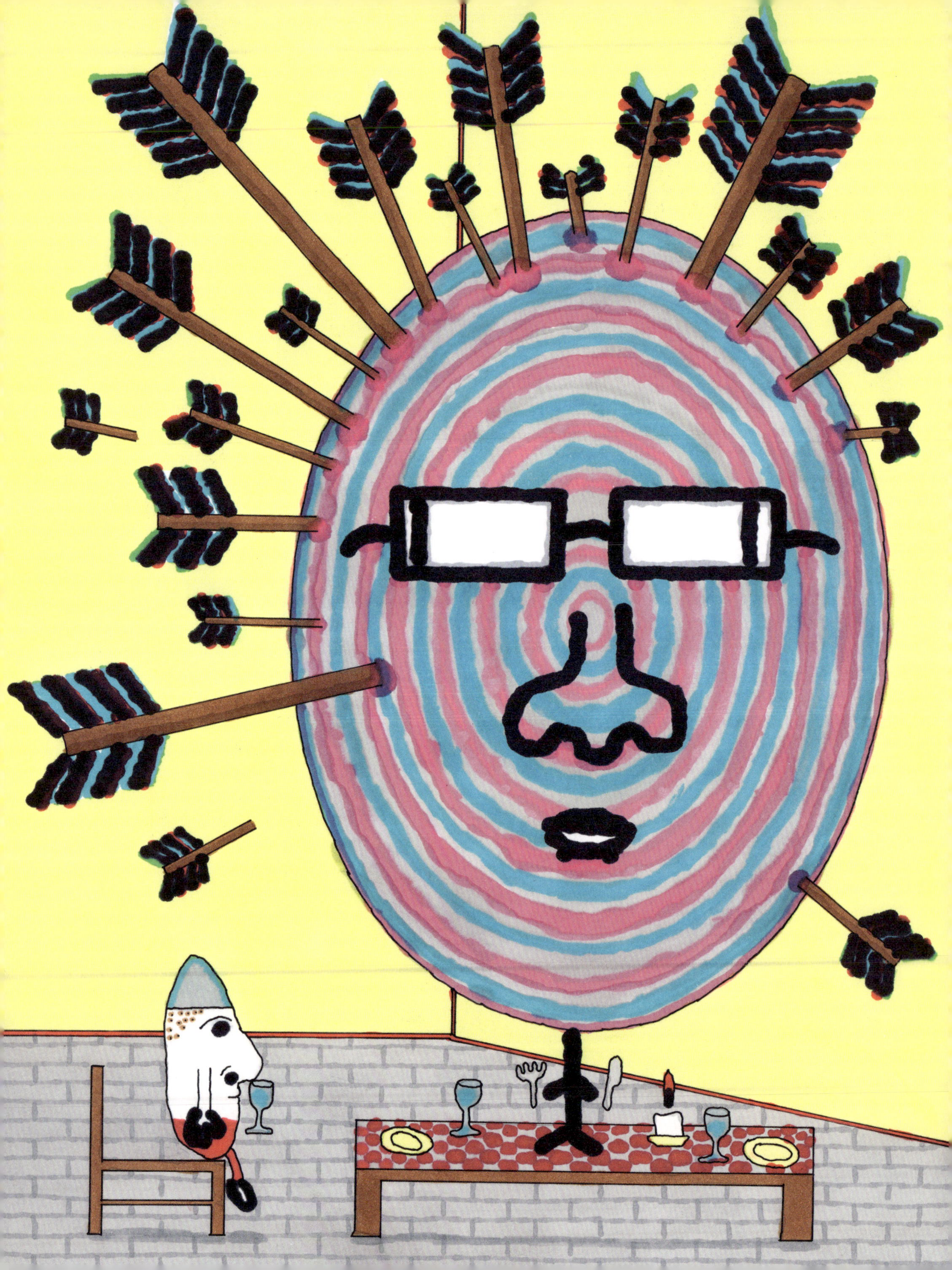

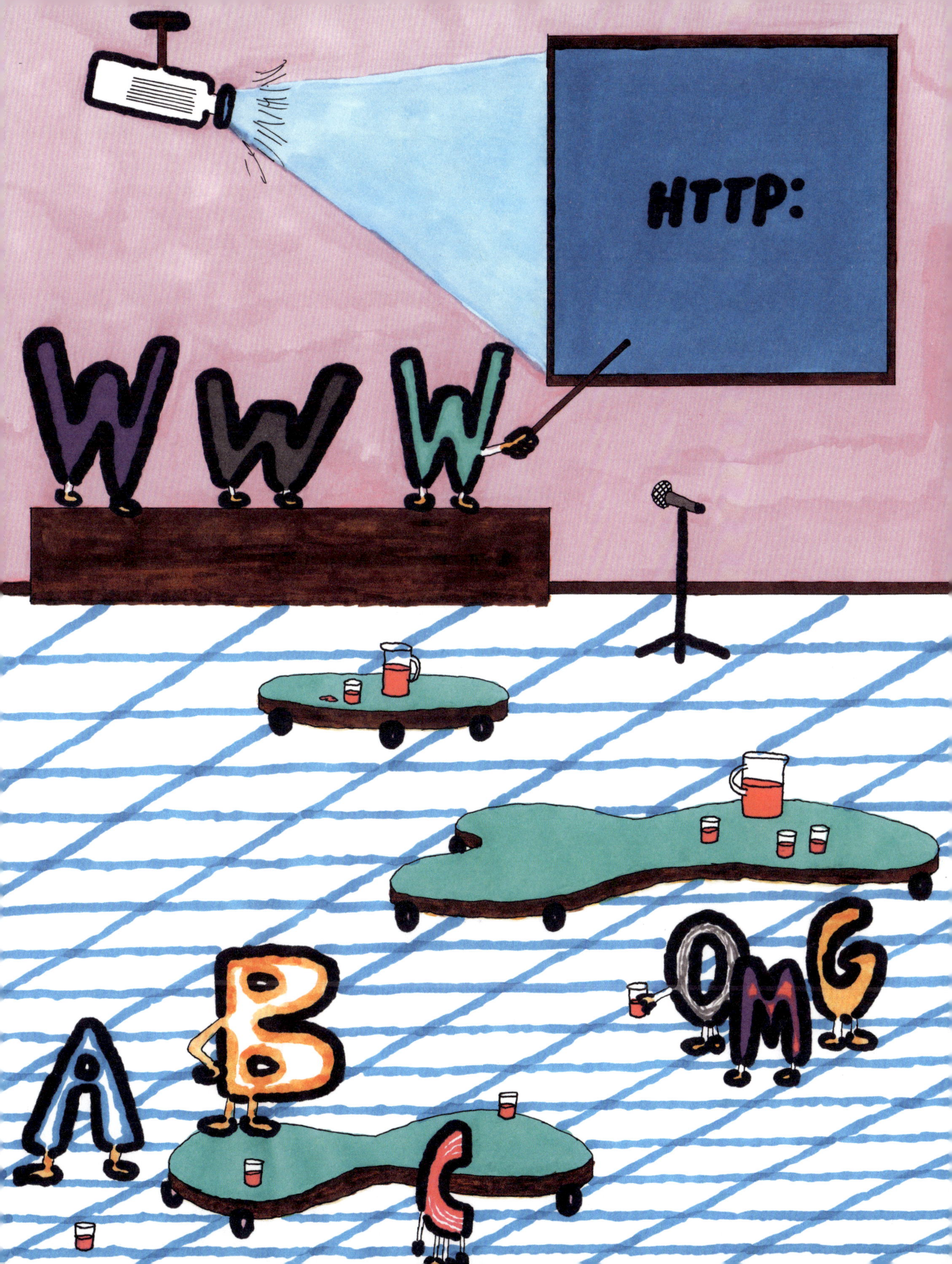
HTTP:

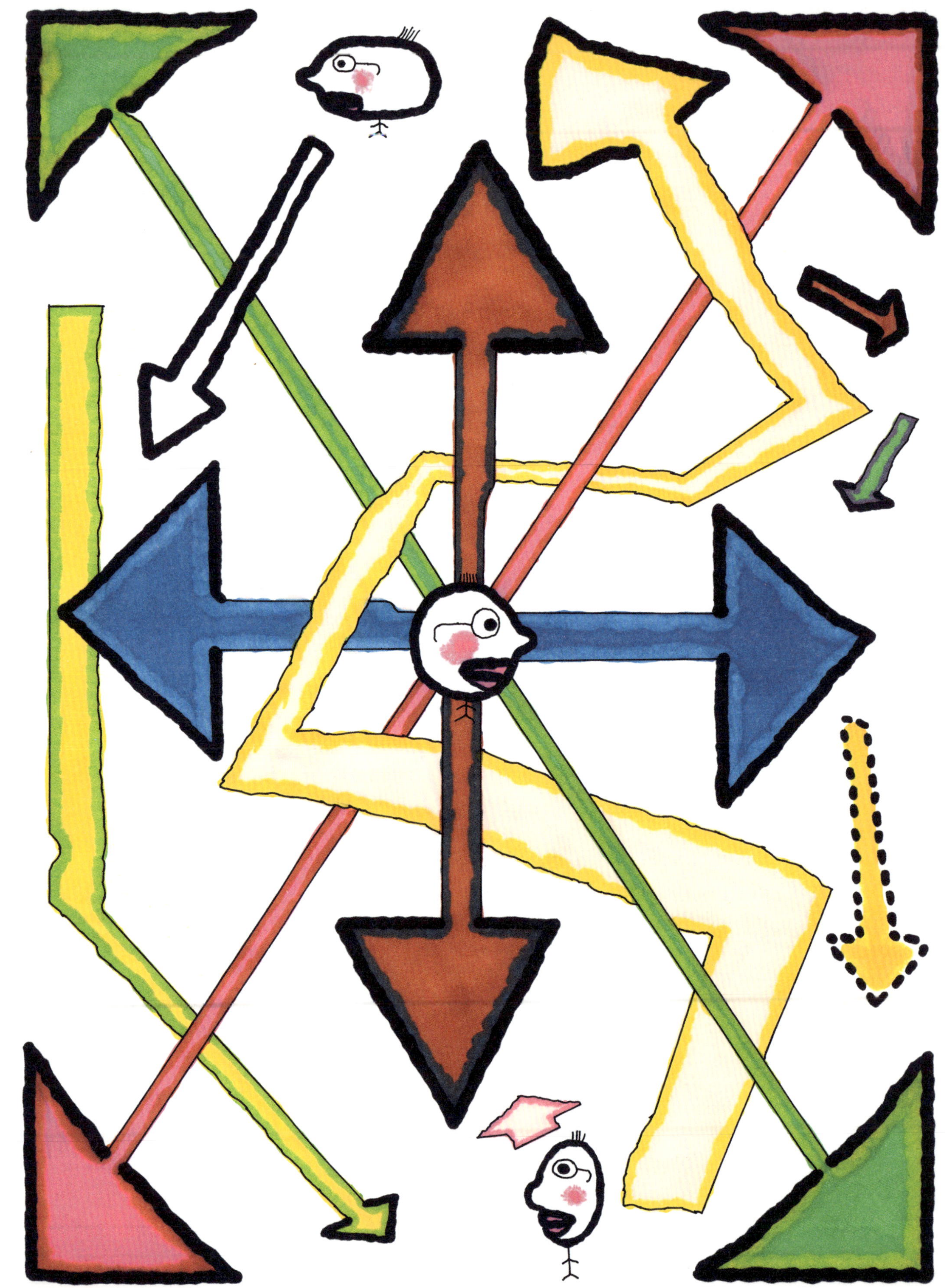

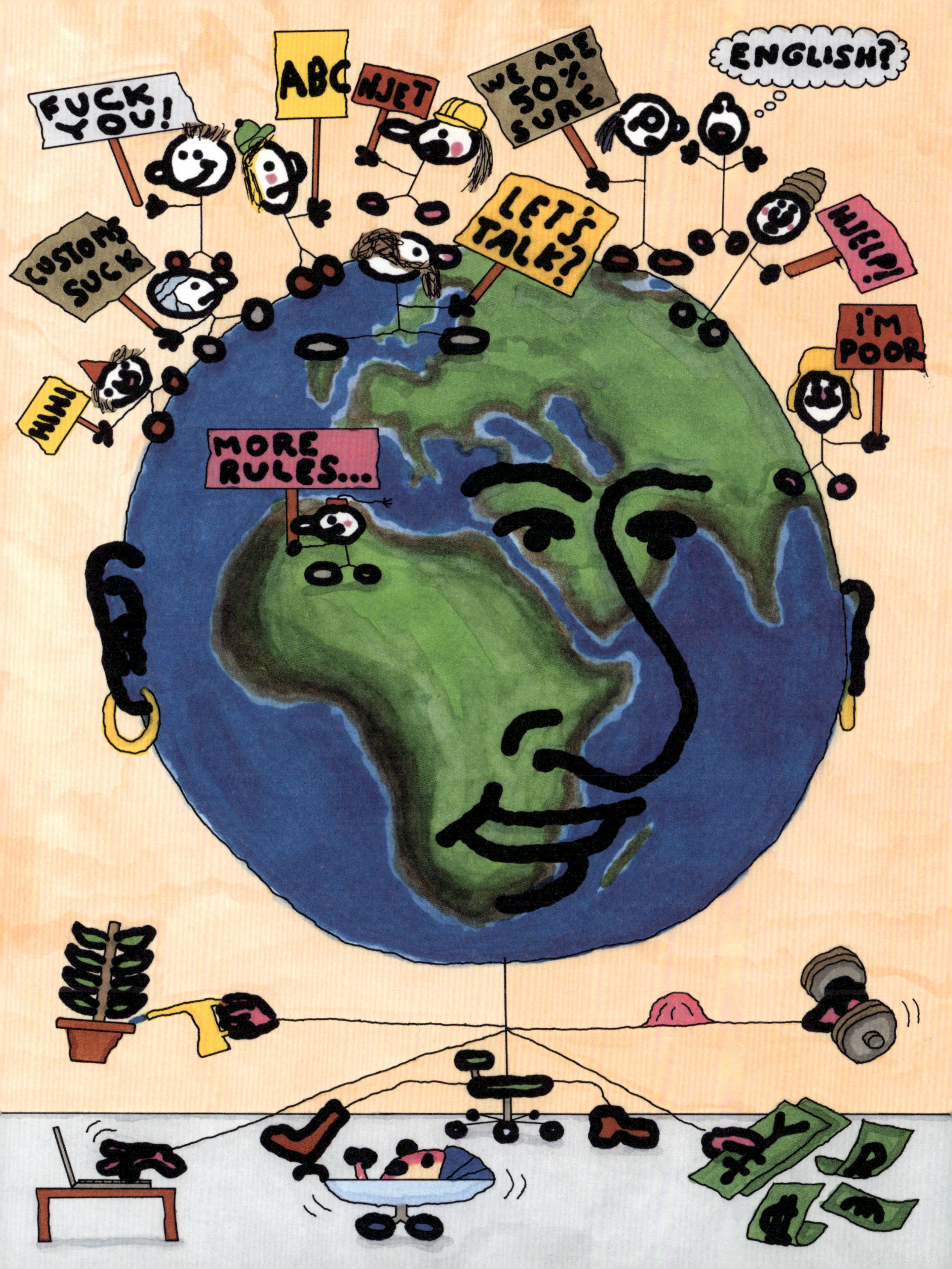
FUCK YOU!
ABC
NJET
WE ARE 50% SURE
ENGLISH?
CUSTOMS SUCK
LET'S TALK?
HELP!
I'M POOR
HIHI
MORE RULES...

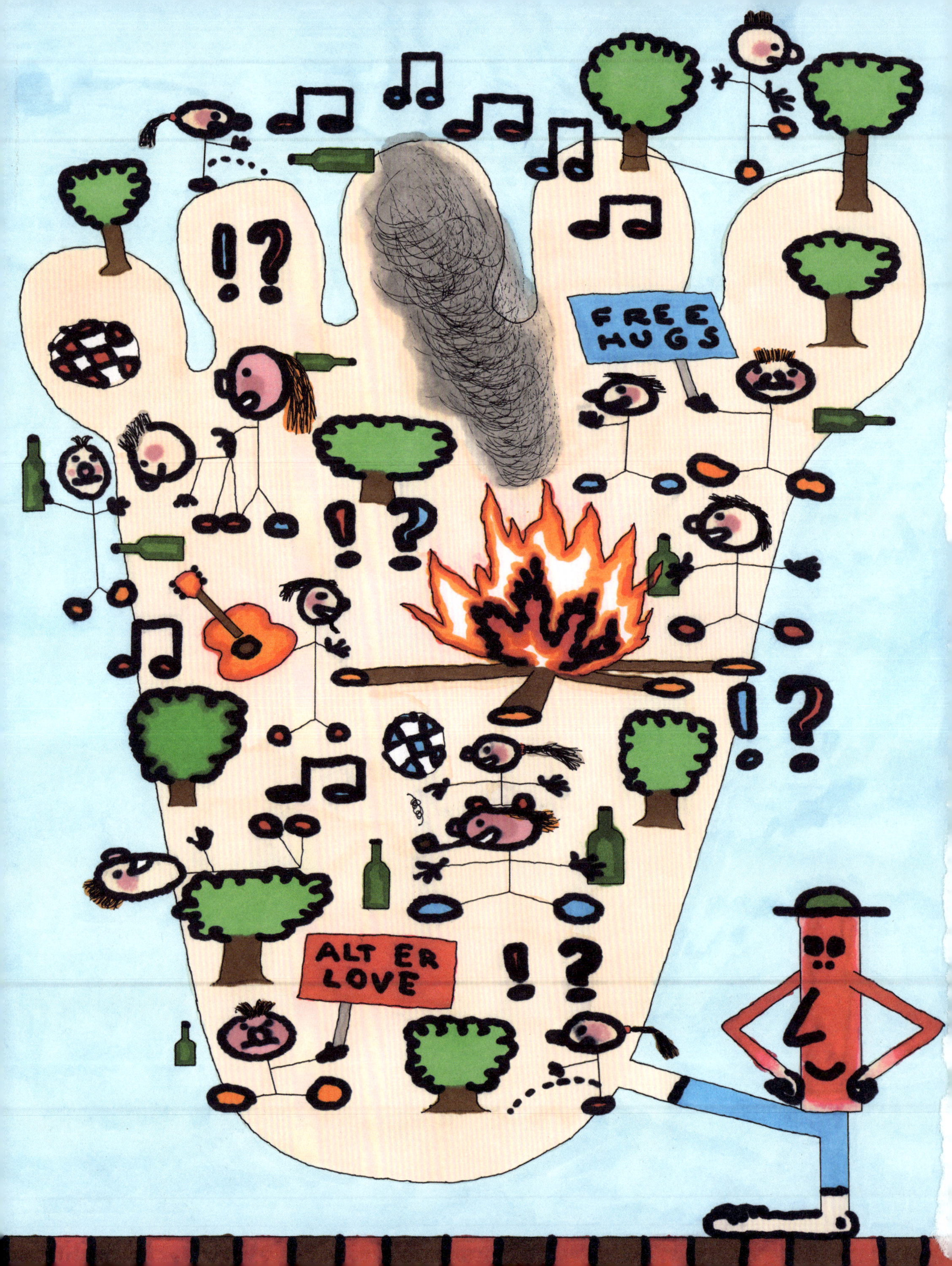
FREE HUGS
ALT ER LOVE